MURDER
— IN —
MICHIGAN'S
UPPER PENINSULA

MURDER
— IN —
MICHIGAN'S
UPPER PENINSULA

SONNY LONGTINE

THE
History
PRESS

Published by The History Press
Charleston, SC 29403
www.historypress.net

Copyright © 2014 by Sonny Longtine
All rights reserved

First published 2014

Manufactured in the United States

ISBN 978.1.62619.355.0

Library of Congress Cataloging-in-Publication Data

Longtine, Sonny.
Murder in Michigan's Upper Peninsula / Sonny Longtine.
pages cm
Includes bibliographical references.
ISBN 978-1-62619-355-0 (paperback)
1. Murder--Michigan--Upper Peninsula--History. 2. Upper Peninsula (Mich.)--Social
conditions. 3. Upper Peninsula (Mich.)--History, Local. 4. Upper Peninsula (Mich.)--
Biography. I. Title.
HV6533.M5L66 2014
364.152'3097749--dc23
2013050155

CONTENTS

Contents

ACKNOWLEDGEMENTS

Writing a book is a formidable task as well as solitary one, but without utilizing the specialized skills of others, this book would have never become a reality.

Victoria Tourtillott did the organization and image editing. Her unequaled attention to detail, particularly with the photographs, enriched the book's presentation. She spent hours bringing old and seemingly unredeemable photographs to life. My never-ending requests for changes she completed with skill and patience. This was always appreciated.

Becky Tavernini skillfully edited the manuscript, ferreting out superfluous language and my never-ending need to editorialize. At times I wrote flourishing whimsical narrations that were excessive and distracted from the story. Becky's editing was clear: less is more. The result is a more tightly written text that quickly flows from page to page.

Judith Greene, an Arizonian, provided the artful sketches. At times she had poor-quality images to work with, but masterfully, she elevated them to print quality.

As always, Jack Deo and Superior View Studio provided me with photographs that I could not have obtained elsewhere.

John Pepin, a *Mining Journal* reporter, who expertly covered the Richardson murder trial, was a tremendous help in providing me with pointers on navigating a courtroom during a trial.

My friend Larry Flanders, a skilled teacher, writer and poet, superbly proofread the manuscript. He and his wife, Astrid, graciously provided

Acknowledgements

shelter and sustenance on several of my research jaunts across the Upper Peninsula.

The following institutions and people contributed to make this book a reality.

Institutions

Bayless Public Library
Beaver Island Historical Society
Houghton Mining Gazette
John Longyear Research Center
Leelanau Historical Society
Marquette Mining Journal
Michigan Technological University Archives/Van Pelt Library
Midland County Historical Society
Ontonagon Historical Society
Peter White Public Library
State of Michigan: Archives of Michigan Photo Collection
Wayne State University: Walter P. Reuther Library

People

Mike Angeli
Karen Bahrman
Kathryn Carlson
William Cashman
Molly Crimmins
Don and Jeanie Culver
Jenette Ellens
Sue Girard/Jackson
Joe and Judy Gregorich
Christine Holland
Jim Humphrey
George Johnson

Bill Jorns
Dave Klimmek
Ellen Kroken
Sister Mary Ann Lauren
Patricia Lundberg
Laverne McDonald
Ann Miller
Karl Numinen
Shirlee Schwemin
John Stevens
Mary Stiles
Heather Sutton

INTRODUCTION

M urderers are supposed to look like murderers.
Surely they must have malicious grimaces; black, smoldering eyes; and menacing expressions that harbor hearts of darkness. Charlie Manson and Attila the Hun look like murderers. We like murderers to be easily identified. But most murderers are not evil appearing; they look no different from you and me.

Early research supported this notion that murderers or criminals could easily be identified by their appearance. At the turn of the century, famed Italian criminologist Cesare Lombroso carefully described the physiology of a criminal: hard, shifty eyes; a large, projecting jaw; a flattened nose; and fleshy lips were physical attributes that Lombroso said were common to criminals. His stereotypical criminal had more of a Neanderthal resemblance than that of modern man. Although his theory of criminal physiognomy has been largely discredited, it nonetheless has a popular following.

What one looks like, however, has little to do with what's in one's heart.

Ted Bundy, John Wilkes Booth and Lawrencia "Bambi" Bembenek hardly looked like murderers, yet juries found them guilty. Ted Bundy was dashing and articulate, yet he murdered thirty-one women. Handsome and charismatic Booth assassinated Abraham Lincoln, and Bambi Bembenek, vivacious and hauntingly beautiful, gunned down her lover's ex-wife.

Murder has many motivations. Greed, jealously, anger, power, insanity, retribution, survival and thrill all provide a basis for murder. Survival murders (spousal abuse) are easier to understand and forgive than those committed by a more sinister motivation. All murders are not equal.

Contrary to public opinion and television, not all murderers are caught. In 2012, Michigan had 689 murders, and many of the perpetrators are still free.

Solving murders is often related to demographics. Of the Michigan murders, 70 percent statewide were solved while only 45 percent were solved in Detroit. Literally "getting away with murder" is more than a trite expression—it happens, in some places more than others. The media reflects the public's interest in murder. Court TV, *Law & Order* and the CSI dramas on television inundate viewers with tales of ghastly murders. Bloody cadavers dissected by pathologists on television are now a common sight.

Michigan's Upper Peninsula is a relatively remote and sparsely populated area, yet its relative remoteness has not prevented murders from occurring. While the per capita rate (five per year) is lower than in many other areas of the state, it nonetheless happens. And the Upper Peninsula fares no better in solving murders than other regions of the state, with 50 percent successfully prosecuted. Isolation does not ensure safety.

The 1967 movie *Bonnie and Clyde*, with Faye Dunaway and Warren Beatty, depicts glamorous, blood-soaked bank bandits as chic and popularized murder as a last resort for the oppressed. Bonnie and Clyde were seen as "bank robbing Robin Hoods" who took from the rich bankers who were the real enemies of the people. Spellbound audiences watched the movie's end, where the protagonists were slaughtered in an orgy of blood and bullets, with sympathy. We abhor murder, but we watch it and read about it with mesmerized detachment.

We are mystified, scared, compelled and absorbed by murder; it is both repelling and alluring. Some murderers are intriguing or mysterious and titillate human curiosity, while others are eccentric, flamboyant egotists or neurotic compulsives.

Public interest in murder is not just a contemporary phenomenon; history is replete with a fascination for murder. The Elizabethans in the 1500s had a curious interest in pamphlets that described the crimes and trials of notorious characters, and executions were an enormous and delightful spectacle.

Perhaps most of us, whether we admit it or not, have had homicidal thoughts. "I could kill him" is a frequent utterance said by many in the fervor of the moment. But it's most often a harmless expression of frustration not acted on. However, it does signify that even the most angelic have entertained thoughts of murder, be it only for a fleeting moment.

1
WHO KILLED JAMES SCHOOLCRAFT?

James Schoolcraft, brother of famous Henry Schoolcraft, was gunned down by an unknown assailant in Sault Ste. Marie in 1846.

Born white but raised by Indians—it has a romantic ring. A white child is spirited away by neighboring Indians and then raised by a tribe that inculcates the white child with Indian skill and wisdom. The captured child becomes one with nature, is strong and courageous and speaks with enlightenment. The hybrid stripling grows into manhood and becomes a bridge binding white and Indian cultures in mutual understanding.

This is the stuff of poetic legends that Kipling or Longfellow might have easily written about. It would make a good movie script, but it is not rooted in reality. The story of John Tanner, a white man raised by Indians, is unique but is one that disdains the romantic notion of successfully blending two markedly different cultures. Tanner was born in 1780 to a Virginia clergyman, Reverend John Tanner Sr. John Senior desired to go west and moved to Kentucky, eventually settling near the mouth of the Big Miami on the Ohio River. It was a dangerous time on the frontier, and native tribes were often hostile to encroaching white men.

John Tanner Jr. was nine years old at the time his parents moved to Kentucky. They were very much aware of their unfriendly surroundings and cautioned the young Tanner not to leave the house. However, as a typical inquisitive and impulsive child, on one occasion he disobeyed his parents and ventured into the yard, where he gathered walnuts. Outside, he was surprised by Indians

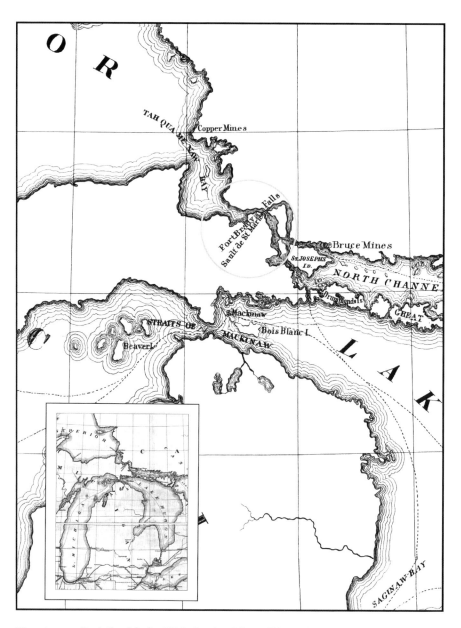

Historic map, Sault Ste. Marie, 1852. *American Library. Library of Congress.*

who snatched him and took him north. All that was left was a pile of nuts, which fell from his hat under the tree. Search parties looking for the kidnapped child never found him. His parents never saw him again.

The Ojibwa kidnappers headed to Detroit and then up the west coast of Lake Huron, where a Native American woman who had recently lost a child of about Tanner's age adopted him. The nomadic tribe moved Tanner from place to place in Michigan. It was not a pleasant experience for him. His adoptive mother treated him decently, but the male members of the family were pitiless. He was starved, beaten and cruelly treated by them. Writers examining Tanner's adult personality described him as morose, sullen and suspicious of others; they attributed this to the harsh treatment he received when growing up.

After years of abuse, a prominent Ottawa woman who lived near where Petoskey is now located purchased him for ten gallons of rum. Tanner's new foster mother held the position of principal chief in the tribe; it was quite unusual for a woman to hold that position in a warlike tribe. By all accounts, his new mother treated him well. Tanner's foster father died a few years after he was adopted.

The family left Petoskey and headed west, eventually settling in Winnipeg, Canada. By now, Tanner had grown into a young man and had taken an Indian wife named "Red-sky-of-the-morning." The union produced three children, one daughter and two sons. One son became a missionary in Canada while the other son was killed in the Second Battle of Bull Run. Tanner had become a skilled hunter and was offered the chieftainship of the tribe, but he turned it down.

Tanner's marriage was unsatisfactory, and he contemplated returning to the United States. His wife was equally unhappy and mulled over suicide. They eventually parted ways.

Always on the move, Tanner eventually returned to northern Michigan and settled in Sault Ste. Marie, where General Lewis Cass hired him as an interpreter. He also acted as an interpreter for various missionary groups and, at times, was employed by fur companies and Indian traders.

Apparently, Tanner was not considered a good father. In 1830, the legislative council of the territory of Michigan passed legislation that authorized the territorial sheriff to remove Martha Tanner from the custody of her father, John Tanner. It was the only time territorial legislation was passed that was specifically written for a private citizen. His daughter was taken to a missionary establishment and eventually became a teacher. After having a productive life, she died on Mackinac Island.

While at the Sault, Tanner got married for the second time to a white Christian woman from Detroit. His second marriage did not fare any better than his first and lasted only a year. The Tanners lived in wretched conditions

Henry Rowe Schoolcraft, ethnologist and famous brother of James Schoolcraft, detested suspected slayer John Tanner. *Superior View Studio.*

in Sault Ste. Marie until Henry Rowe Schoolcraft, a famous Indian ethnologist, and some friends rescued Mrs. Tanner from the pathetic hovel and secured passage for her on a boat back to Detroit. She was relieved to get away from her miserable existence with Tanner.

In 1846, the shaggy-haired and unattractive Tanner was sixty-six years of age, and his life was about to take a turn for the worse. He was accused of killing Henry Schoolcraft's brother, James. In August of that year, it was purported that Tanner had gunned down James Schoolcraft near Fort Brady in the Sault. Records indicate that Schoolcraft was walking from his residence at the fort and down a path toward a field he had been clearing. Dense bushes fringed the path where the assassin lay in waiting. Although Schoolcraft was a strong, athletic man, in the prime of life, he was not a match for the one-ounce ball and number three buckshot that ripped through his body. After he was hit, he apparently vaulted forward with a huge leap and exited out of his slippers, leaving them intact and together on the walkway. It was reported that Tanner had been on a rampage for several days prior to the murder and had just burned down his own house. Tanner was said to have remarked earlier, "I had yet to deal with two or three of the citizens of Sault Ste. Marie."

If Tanner murdered Schoolcraft, it was never proven. After the murder, Tanner disappeared and was never heard from again.

Several stories examine why Tanner would want to kill Schoolcraft. It was speculated that he was angrier with Henry Schoolcraft than he was with James, but apparently James was an easier target. And what better revenge could there be than to murder Henry's brother? When Henry was the Indian agent at the Sault, it is conjectured that he had rebuffed Tanner and that the murder of his brother was Tanner's way of getting even for not only this but also for arranging transport for Tanner's second wife's escape. Tanner never forgot that. Just prior to Schoolcraft's murder, Tanner remarked with bitterness, "Nobody will live with me; here I have lived alone for years—everybody has left me—they have taken away my children, my furniture, everything I had and left me without anything…everybody is my enemy, and it's all owing to Henry Schoolcraft."

Henry believed to his dying day that Tanner had killed his brother. He said, "This lawless vagabond waylaid and shot my brother James, having concealed himself in a cedar thicket." In a continuing bitter commentary of Tanner, Schoolcraft vehemently spewed, "He [Tanner] is now a gray-headed, hard featured, old man, whose feelings are at war with everyone on earth, white or red."

Another theory concerned Tanner's daughter and the attention James Schoolcraft was paying to her. A conjecture that an army lieutenant was the killer was also in the Sault rumor mill. Lieutenant Bryant P. Tilden, an army officer at Fort Brady, was said to harbor bitter feelings toward Schoolcraft over a rift they had over a woman, and some said that he killed Schoolcraft. The buck and ball cartridge used in the murder was military issue and gave this theory further validity. Speculation was that Tilden was aware that Tanner was in the vicinity when he shot Schoolcraft. For Tilden, this was a fortuitous occurrence and made it easy for him to cast the blame on a suspicious and unlikable Tanner. It was rumored that after killing Schoolcraft, Tilden returned to Fort Brady and told his superior officers that he saw Tanner in the area of the Schoolcraft shooting.

Tanner was an easy mark for someone to blame. After all, he was known as a loose cannon, and just the day before the murder, he had burned down his home. Ironically, Tilden was put in charge of a party to hunt down Tanner. They never found him. Shortly after the murder, Tilden was transferred to fight in the Mexican War. Reportedly, he made a deathbed confession some years later that he had killed Schoolcraft.

Depending on whom you believe, Tanner was variously depicted. Some saw him as surly, uncommunicative, treacherous and a dangerous savage; however, others extolled his virtues and saw him as noble man with generous qualities and trustworthy Indian ethics, one of which was his honest intercourse with traders.

As an adult, Tanner was a lonely man caught between two worlds, to neither of which he belonged. Prior to his disappearance from the Sault, he lived in a small cabin by himself and had limited contact with others.

What happened to John Tanner? No one knows for sure. One possibility is that he died in a swamp near the Sault. A handgun and a rifle found in the swamp near skeletal remains were identified as belonging to Tanner. Perhaps it was Tanner, but more than likely, it will remain an unsolved mystery.

> *The most Indian thing about the Indians is not his moccasins or his calumet, his wampum or his stone hatchet, but traits of character and sagacity, skill, or passion.*
>
> —*Ralph Waldo Emerson*

2
THE INTOLERABLE TORMENTOR

Quiet August Pond was repeatedly bullied by village fishermen until he could take no more.

A majestic white, conical tower soars seventy-eight feet heavenward. Ornate brackets support the tower's graceful lantern crown. Billowy clouds gently buffet the tower and then lazily float on. The tower's base securely rests on a grassy field not far from Lake Michigan. The grass yields to tender winds that sweep across the small cape jutting into the lake. This is Seul Choix (pronounced "sis-shwa," a French expression meaning "only choice"), where a much-needed lighthouse was built in 1895. It is the only lighthouse on a seventy-five-mile stretch on northern Lake Michigan between St. Ignace and Manistique. This idyllic setting draws tourists who climb the tower, walk the expansive grass, stroll the sandy beach and enjoy the serenity of the peaceful point on warm summer days.

In the early 1600s, Seul Choix was a favorite place for Native Americans who sought whitefish and lake trout, which teemed in the offshore waters. French fur traders and immigrants followed the Native Americans to the fishing site and established a small community on the promontory. By 1850, it was a village replete with a trading store.

But in 1859, all was not well in the restful setting. Rancor, anger and murder now permeated the fishing hamlet.

August Pond was a quiet fisherman who lived the good life in the village with his wife and three children. The eldest child was twelve years old while the youngest was an infant. They lived in a shanty that was more shack than

Fishing was the economic livelihood at Seul Choix, a diminutive community on the north shore of Lake Michigan, located just east of Manistique. *Superior View Studio*.

house; it had one door, one window and a bark roof. The room was crowded with three people in its 256 square feet. The flimsy wood door had only an inside rope latch for security.

Adjacent to Pond's house was a fishing net house that he owned. Two fishermen, Daniel Whitney and Dennis Cull, occupied it. The fishermen were employed by Pond and used the net house as their sleeping quarters. Whitney and Cull ate their meals with the Ponds, and the group functioned much like an extended family. Pond was an industrious man content to quietly go his own way.

David Plant, Isaac Blanchard and Joseph Robilliard were fisherman who also lived in the hamlet. They were the village bullies, and Plant was the most belligerent of the three. They had it in for Pond, and for one week in June 1859, they unmercifully harassed him. There wasn't any reason to harass Pond, but it was evident they immensely disliked him and humiliated him whenever they had a chance.

Plant, while at the residence of a Mrs. Downy, said, "I must whip Pond or there would be a fracas." Later in the week, Plant, Blanchard and Robilliard confronted Pond and threatened him. Plant told Pond that "he did not use his neighbor's right; that they ought not to pick on men not of his size and abuse them, and if Pond wanted to fight anybody, he had better take a man of his size." Plant's threats were without any provocation by Pond. During the conversation, Plant hit Pond on his face, knocked his hat off with the blow and then kicked him. Pond did not retaliate but picked up his hat, put it on and ran off into the woods.

Later that evening, Plant, Robilliard and Blanchard broke into Pond's net house and demanded a startled and sleeping Whitney to tell them where Pond was. Whitney told Plant that he didn't know. Plant never told Whitney why he wanted to see Pond. The vigilante trio then went to Pond's house and terrified Mrs. Pond. She knew they were up to no good and had been harassing her husband. She told the intruders that he was not there. Pond, fearing for his life, never returned home that evening but stayed at a neighbor's house.

The following day, Plant and his collaborators were again on the prowl for Pond. They found him near Peter Closs's residence and made more threats. "It's a good while since you have a grudge against me; I must whip to satisfy myself," Plant hostilely told Pond. Again, Pond did not respond to the bullying; he quietly went home.

That night, after drinking on a fishing boat, and between one and two o'clock in the morning, Plant, Robilliard and Blanchard went to Pond's net house and began to tear the roof off. From there, they went to Pond's house and banged on the door. Again, a frightened Mrs. Pond told Plant that her husband wasn't there. Plant demanded she get some sugar for his whiskey. She complied and slid him sugar through a crack in the door. Meanwhile, an intimidated and petrified August Pond was hiding under the bed and fearing for his life.

The rabble-rousing threesome then went to neighbor (and Pond's cousin) Peter Ward's house, where they raised hell. Plant told Ward, "I want to see Gust Pond; he abused an Irishman, and I want to abuse him just as bad as he abused the Irishman." In all probability, Plant's rhetoric was made up to justify his tyranny. The threesome went back to Pond's house, where again, Mrs. Pond denied them entry, and they continued to tear down the net house. Plant jumped on a panicked Cull and began to choke him, demanding to know where Pond was. Cull was terrorized, but he did not respond.

In the meantime, Pond went to Peter Closs's home and retrieved a loaded double-barreled shotgun. Closs was a nearby neighbor and Pond's cousin. Upon returning to his house, Pond saw Plant and his collaborators tearing down his net house; he finally mustered enough courage to face his tormentors. He told them, "Leave or I'll shoot." They contemptuously ignored his demand and continued to tear down the net house. With confidence and in a strong voice, again, Pond again told them to leave. They didn't.

It was near daybreak, and the sun was just peeking over the horizon when a burst from a discharging shotgun resonated throughout the community. Pellets from the shotgun hit Isaac Blanchard. He staggered several hundred yards to a small path near some bushes and died.

Shortly after the killing, Pond turned himself in to Louis Pond, his brother, who was the village constable. Louis Pond was confused and unsure of what to do—so he did nothing. An exasperated August Pond then sought the help of his two hired hands, Whitney and Cull, to take him to Beaver Island, where Pond planned to turn himself over to the island authorities. The three began the twenty-five-mile rowboat journey early on Saturday morning. A revengeful Plant and his cohorts didn't want Pond to go to Beaver Island; they wanted him jailed and tried at Mackinac Island. As a result, Plant and four others pursued Pond across Lake Michigan. They caught Pond's boat seven miles from Beaver Island. After Pond's capture, they took him to Mackinac Island.

Pond's attorney in his trial presented a case of self-defense. At the time, however, the argument that one was justified in killing someone who was threatening one's home was not yet recognized by the courts. As a result, Pond was convicted of manslaughter and sentenced to ten years in prison.

Unhappy with the result, Pond's attorneys appealed the case to the Michigan Supreme Court. The attorneys felt there were sufficient grounds for a ruling of justifiable homicide. In 1860, the court heard Pond's case that advocated justifiable homicide. The court agreed with the position that the killing was justifiable and threw out the lower court's decision. The Michigan Supreme Court broadened the justifiable defense position and stated, "A man assaulted in his dwelling is not obligated to retreat, but may use such means as is absolutely necessary to repel the assailant from his house." As a result, a new trial was ordered for August Pond. Unfortunately, Pond died before his second trial, though in all probability he would have been exonerated of murder. This Michigan Supreme Court ruling, nevertheless, was a landmark decision that not only expanded the right of self-defense in Michigan but also influenced the national legal system.

Pond, an uneducated fisherman from an isolated fishing community, never lived to know how he played a pivotal role in Michigan law. He lived in a shanty, was a decent man and in death proclaimed to the world that a "man's home is indeed his castle."

The Mackinac Island courthouse was the county seat in 1859 when August Pond was tried for murder. In 1882, when St. Ignace became the county seat, the old courthouse was abandoned. *Shirly Schwemin.*

In 1995, a bronze plaque was placed outside the Mackinac Island courthouse and dedicated to the 1860 landmark decision.

Seul Choix, as a village, has vanished, and it is no longer a fishing port. Local fishermen, however, still extensively commercially fish the coastal waters. In 2005, 400,000 pounds of fish were harvested from the lake.

Pond is long gone, but the fishing that was his life's mainstay 140 years ago still thrives and continues to support coastal families in Michigan's Upper Peninsula.

3
VIGILANTE HANGINGS

Frontier justice in the Upper Peninsula in the 1880s resulted in two Menominee loggers swinging from a rope in the town center.

In 1880, Menominee was the lumber port capital of the world and home to a rugged lot: lumberjacks— tough, crude men—who worked hard during the week and raised hell on the weekends.

Two of the lumberjacks were Frank and John McDonald. The McDonald cousins were from Nova Scotia, Canada, and had a reputation as bad men, particularly when they were drunk—which was all too frequent.

The McDonalds repeatedly caused disturbances at the lumber camp. On one occasion, Sheriff Julius Reprecht was sent up to the lumber camp where the McDonalds were in the midst of a donnybrook. When Reprecht attempted to quash the disturbance, Frank McDonald, the younger of the two cousins, took offense to the sheriff's interference and pulverized the hapless man unconscious.

> *The mob is man voluntarily descending to the nature of the beast*
> —*Ralph Waldo Emerson.*

Shortly after the beating, Deputy Sheriff Billy Kittson, a burly two-hundred-pound man, arrested and jailed the McDonalds. They were tried, convicted and sentenced to one and a half years at the Jackson State Prison. They served their time uneventfully and were released early for good

A drunken vigilante mob hanged the McDonald cousins on a tree in downtown Menominee for the killing of Deputy Sheriff Bill Kittson. *Menominee County Historical Society.*

behavior. They returned to Menominee, where they resumed their old ways: working during the day and drinking and raising Cain at night.

One night, the McDonalds began drinking at the Montreal House, a bar in Frenchtown. The bartender on duty was Norman Kittson, brother of the deputy sheriff who was responsible for the McDonalds' incarceration. The McDonalds let Norman Kittson know they were out to even the score with his brother. After a short stay at the Montreal House, the McDonalds paid a visit to the Three Chimney House, a nearby and well-known house of prostitution. Fortuitously, the brothers ran across their old nemesis, Billy Kittson. The "ladies" immediately began to shower attention on the McDonald boys. This angered Kittson, and a mêlèe ensued with Kittson hitting Frank McDonald over the head with a bottle and then leaving the Three Chimney House.

The vengeful McDonalds followed Kittson to the street, where John McDonald clubbed him with a heavy, metal pipe. Not satisfied with dropping him to his knees, McDonald then plunged a six-inch dagger into his back. Kittson's brother, Norman, witnessing the brawl, sped to his rescue, but a McDonald stabbed him. Billy Kittson, wounded and bleeding profusely, got back into the fray to help his beleaguered brother. Norman pulled out a gun and shot Frank in the leg. Billy, the life blood draining out of him, feebly staggered to the Montreal House, where he gasped his last breath and fell over dead in the street.

With the blood bath now concluded, the McDonalds seized a nearby horse and buggy and went directly to Dr. P.T. Phillips, who attended to their wounds. After getting medical treatment, they quickly departed north to Cedar River. On the way, they were arrested and jailed by David Barclay, the new Menominee sheriff.

Judge Henry Nason attempted to have a court inquest the next day, but he wisely decided to forgo the proceeding when he learned the citizens of the community were in a rage over the murder the McDonalds had committed. Nason felt that by delaying the inquest he would defuse a potentially explosive situation, a decision he would come to regret.

> *The mob rides an emotional roller coaster and is always on the brink of shedding blood or tears.*
>
> —*Anonymous*

On Monday, the *Marinette Eagle* speculated on the "serious threats of lynching the McDonalds," but the night passed without any further violence.

Odgen Avenue in downtown Menominee in the 1890s. The McDonald cousins were beaten and kicked as they were dragged down this street. *Menominee County Historical Society.*

But on Tuesday, it turned ugly. Local men gathered at the Forvilly House, a large hotel and saloon, and plied themselves with liquor. By evening, the drunken rabble had decided that lynching the McDonald boys was the surest and quickest way to have justice. Armed with liquor and self-righteousness, the angry vigilante band marched down the street to the jail and demanded the McDonalds.

When the rabid mob was denied the McDonalds, it grabbed a telegraph pole, and cursing wildly, smashed open the entry door. After a brief scuffle, the deputies were subdued and the McDonalds forced out of their jail cell and clubbed with an axe. With brute force they were taken out of the jail.

A local priest, Father Heliard, unsuccessfully attempted to stop the mob; the members of the pack cursed and spat on the priest and pushed him into the gutter. The lynch party tied one end of the rope around the McDonalds' necks and the other end to a horse and buggy and then dragged them down Odgen Avenue. Then, the participants savagely jumped up and down on the defenseless bodies, ripping off flesh with their lumberjack boots.

Pandemonium spread as a gathering crowd along the route hurled rocks and garbage and cursed the McDonalds. When the lynch party approached an intersection with a railroad crossing, having spent its energy, it decided the area was a good place to hang the McDonalds. The vigilantes hoisted the two men onto a railroad crossing sign with ropes around their necks and then left the carnage of their handiwork for eager spectators to view. The McDonalds were dead long before they were hanged from the sign.

The mob, still in a drunken rage, took the bodies down from the crossing sign and hauled them to a brothel on Belview Avenue. In a further act of debauchery, the necktie party forced a prostitute to lie with the dead McDonalds. Then they burned down the brothel and hanged the cousins from a nearby jack pine.

The next day, the McDonalds were still hanging from the tree next to the smoldering rubble of the prostitution house. The drunken frenzy was over.

A jury indicted several leaders of the mob for murder, but nothing ever came of it. Charges were dismissed for various reasons. One man did eventually go to trial but was found not guilty. No one was ever convicted of the McDonalds' murders.

When justice is denied, does it seek other avenues to express itself? Perhaps it did in the McDonald case, as several of the men suspected of being involved in the lynching also met violent deaths:

Albert Beach, a log driver, fell out of his boat and drowned.

Louis Porter died after apparently being bitten by a rattlesnake.

A mill owner was fatally injured in a lumberyard fire.

A witness named Dunn was later cut in two by a sawmill.

In the 1930s, a Federal Employment project renovated the old jail that housed the McDonalds. Bloodstains left from the infamous day over fifty years earlier were clearly visible in the McDonald cell—a reminder of a past when justice in a frontier Upper Peninsula town retreated into the murky depths of mob vigilantism.

The McDonalds are buried in an unmarked grave in the potter's field section of the Riverside Cemetery.

4
STAGECOACH STICKUP

WANTED FOR ROBBERY AND MURDER: REIMUND (REINHARDT) HOLZHEY—REWARD $2,800. CONTACT SHERIFF DAVID FOLEY, BESSEMER, AUGUST 27, 1889.

Y ou'll get nothing out of me," a defiant Arnold Macarcher said to Reimund Holzhey who had a .44-caliber side arm jammed into his abdomen. With that, the angry Macarcher pulled out the revolver he had hidden inside his coat and fired at Holzhey, who was attempting to rob him. Macarcher's errant shot went wide and missed his attacker. Twenty-two-year-old Holzhey responded with a volley from his handgun. One of his shots hit Macarcher in the mouth, seriously wounding him. Macarcher was one of four passengers on a stagecoach near Bessemer in the western Upper Peninsula.

In the ensuing confusion, the frightened stagecoach horses bolted and careened down the road. Reimund Holzhey blazed away with his six guns at the departing stage. Two shots hit passenger Adolph Fleischbein in the abdomen, sending him toppling off the stagecoach and crashing to the earth. Two frightened female passengers screamed in horror as they watched the bloody mêlèe. Fleischbein was dead, and Macarcher was seriously wounded.

This was the last stagecoach robbery in Michigan. It took place in 1889 on an isolated and primitive stretch of road that ran from the Gogebic Station to the plush Lake Gogebic resorts that were close to the town of Bessemer. It was ideal for a robbery. Highwayman Holzhey knew what he was doing. Both Macarcher and Fleischbein were bankers and probably carrying a good deal of cash. He thought it would be "easy pickin's"; after all, he had just finished several successful heists in northern Wisconsin and Upper Michigan. Holzhey didn't think the robbery would end up with him committing murder and having the law hot on his trail.

Reimund Holzhey was a transient German immigrant who had just migrated to the Bessemer area from Milwaukee; he went there believing there were riches to be found in the Gogebic Range. He was bright but uneducated, didn't have any job skills and didn't get along with people. Rumors of gold, silver and diamonds in the Gogebic area lured Holzhey

Reimund Holzhey, stagecoach robber and murderer. *Judith (Suavnto) Greene.*

Republic as it appeared in the late 1890s. Reimund Holzhey was captured here after a botched stagecoach heist. Republic, at the time, was a booming mining community. *Superior View Studio.*

into the belief that quick riches were soon to be his. He just needed a stake. For Holzhey, robbery was the easiest and quickest way to get his stake.

After the robbery debacle, he scampered off into the woods with his ill-gotten booty. He lived in the woods for the next several days, eating berries and begging meals from unsuspecting fishermen and campers whom he encountered along the way. After several days of this nomadic existence, he hopped a train to Republic, some one hundred miles from the scene of his holdup.

In Republic, Holzhey's crime spree came to an end. Vigilante law officials from the small mining community would unceremoniously capture the desperado with a price on his head. Historic records vary as to how the actual apprehension took place—some descriptions more colorful but perhaps less accurate than others.

One newspaper account of the nabbing of Holzhey comes close to describing the Gunfight at the O.K. Corral. The article states that Holzhey stepped out of his hotel in Republic on a bright sunny morning, only to be quickly surrounded by an angry mob. The law officers subdued him just before he could reach for his gun, and then he was kicked unconscious by a self-righteous rabble that demanded his immediate lynching. He survived the capture and was incarcerated briefly in Republic and then sent to Bessemer for trial.

The twenty-one-year-old Holzhey was tried in Bessemer's Circuit Court in October 1889. His trial garnered the most attention

A youthful and seemingly unconcerned Reimund Holzhey (center) is handcuffed and guarded by a well-armed sheriff. The German immigrant with an unpleasant personality thought robbing was an easy way to get rich. *Superior View Studio.*

in the community, even though it was competing with the town's most colorful prostitute on trial for selling whiskey and a local judge being litigated for embezzlement. The Holzhey incarceration was drawing so much attention that the local sheriff decided to capitalize on the media frenzy by agreeing to have Holzhey photographed in a local studio, wearing a macho ammunition vest and toting a long rifle. The sheriff, with entrepreneurial adroitness, sold the pictures to the curious as well as to souvenir seekers. Young children were shown the photograph of the ominous-looking Holzhey and told in stern terms that bad things happen to children who don't obey their parents.

The twelve-man jury convicted Holzhey in forty-five minutes in spite of his defensive plea that he had "unnatural feelings" and spells of amnesia after a horse had kicked him in the head. Playing the "victim" card in 1889 did little good, and he was sentenced to a life term at the Marquette Branch Prison.

Holzhey served twenty-four years in prison for his crime. Prison records reported that Holzhey had recovered from his criminal tendencies following surgery that removed a bone splinter lodged in his brain. He was a model prisoner, eventually becoming the head prison librarian and editor of the penitentiary paper.

Upon his release in 1913, he took a job as a guide for the exclusive Huron Mountain Club, a posh retreat for the wealthy, just north of Marquette. He worked there for the next twenty years, and then at the age of sixty-three, he moved to Florida and began a new career as a freelance writer.

Throughout most of his adult life, Holzhey complained of severe headaches and nightmares. Whether these recurring terrible dreams had anything to do with a conscience weary of forty-three years of guilt over the murder he committed is unclear, but one thing is certain: at the age of eighty-six, he took his own life by putting a bullet through his brain while sitting quietly on a rocking chair on his back porch.

5

WHEN DEATH COMES AT DARK

Molly Beveridge, a new bride, was slain in the village of Matchwood in 1889.

In 1895, Jack McDonald was released from the Marquette Branch Prison after serving five years for the murder of Molly Beveridge. Beveridge was murdered in Matchwood, thirty miles south of Ontonagon on M-28 in the western Upper Peninsula, in 1889. Eyewitnesses to the murder were James Redpath and Duncan Beveridge, McDonald's housemates. A jury believed Redpath and Beveridge and convicted a hapless McDonald of murder. McDonald was released from prison when new information came to light that McDonald was duped into believing he committed the murder, when in reality, Beveridge and Redpath were responsible for the killing.

At the time of the murder, James Redpath, Maggie Flaherty, Duncan Beveridge, Molly Beveridge and James McDonald were sharing a small house in Matchwood. Today, Matchwood is an unincorporated community with a population of 115. The town was named after the area's largest employer, the Diamond Match Company. Their home, with slightly over five hundred square feet, was cramped, and living conditions were far from ideal for the two couples and McDonald. The Beverages had just been married. Redpath and the twenty-one-year-old Maggie Flaherty were not married but living together.

The house was built by McDonald but later sold to Redpath. Rumors circulated at the time that Redpath did not purchase the home from McDonald but won it in a poker game. Sleeping accommodations were far from desirable. The couples partitioned off one end of the house into two eight- by eight-foot cubicles, which served as sleeping quarters. The Beveridges hung a curtain at the end of their cubicle, providing them with a modicum of privacy. Redpath and Flaherty, apparently without a need of privacy, did not curtain their cubicle.

McDonald bought property near the Redpath house and was planning on building a new house. He was a burly logger and offered his haying services to Redpath in exchange for a place to live. Redpath and the other house occupants agreed to the terms, and McDonald moved in. Far from an ideal arrangement, a cot was set up in the kitchen at night for McDonald. The ladies, somewhat apprehensive about having a rugged bachelor occupy the house, kept the door latched between the kitchen and their "bedrooms."

In spite of the congested living conditions, all seemed to be working out for McDonald and the young couples. The ladies took care of the household chores and then assisted Redpath and Beveridge in haying.

The harmony was shattered on the night of November 11, 1889, when all hell broke loose. Molly Beveridge was shot and killed, and Maggie Flaherty was seriously wounded. McDonald was held accountable for the evening's bloodshed.

Beveridge and Redpath testified against McDonald at his trial. The duo contended that McDonald broke from his bedroom (kitchen) in the middle of the night and began to wildly shoot, killing Molly Beveridge and severely wounding Flaherty. Duncan Beveridge and Redpath easily convinced McDonald that he had committed the murders. They told McDonald that he was sleepwalking when he did it. A compliant and befuddled McDonald, who was easily duped, agreed that he must have done it, although he said he couldn't remember. No motive was attached to the killing. At the trial, McDonald's attorney used sleepwalking as his client's defense, but to no avail. McDonald was convicted and sent to prison for five years

McDonald's attorney did not have any forensics to refute the witness testimony, thus making the conviction of McDonald a slam-dunk.

However, this was not the end of the case. In 1895, Flaherty told a new version of events that occurred in 1889. Five years after the murder, Flaherty, now twenty-eight, with an apparent desire to clear her conscience, said that Duncan Beveridge and James Redpath were the ones who killed Molly Beveridge. According to Flaherty's new story, she was awakened at 2:30 a.m. by the sound of the Beveridges rowdily bickering. She heard Molly say, "I'm going away, and when I get away, I'm going to fix you plenty." Flaherty said there was a pause, then the sound of footsteps and then a gunshot.

Flaherty said she left the bedroom and approached a dimly lit sitting room, where she heard the shot. When she entered the room, she saw Duncan Beveridge with a Winchester rifle in his hand, standing near his wife's prostrate and bloody body.

An alarmed Beveridge saw Flaherty enter the room, aimed his gun at her and fired, hitting her in the thigh with a life-threatening wound. Redpath, hearing all the commotion, rushed into the sitting room to find one person dead and another seriously wounded. A panicked Redpath screamed at Beveridge, "My God, Duncan, what have you done?" The din awakened McDonald, and he attempted to open the latched kitchen door, but to no avail. Beveridge yelled through the door that he was just shooting at some lynx through an open window. A naïve and somewhat intellectually limited McDonald believed Beveridge and remained in his kitchen/bedroom. According to Flaherty, Beveridge and Redpath decided to hang the murder on an unsuspecting and easily hoodwinked McDonald. McDonald was then called out of the bedroom and told that he must have committed the crime, but he was probably sleepwalking when he did it.

The devious duo then continued with the crime cover-up by tossing the injured Flaherty into bed and telling her to keep her mouth shut or she, too, would be in trouble. Fearing retribution from Beveridge and Redpath, Flaherty kept quiet for years. The gunshot wound to Flaherty resulted in a broken leg, and it required a year's hospitalization in Marquette.

Why Flaherty came forth with a new version of the murder is not clear. Beyond an attempt to clear her conscience, Flaherty may have sought revenge for the bad treatment she received from Beveridge and Redpath. After she was released from the hospital, she rejoined Redpath and Beveridge in Menominee in their latest business venture—a brothel. Sources said that Maggie Flaherty was drunk much of the time and caused trouble with the other "working girls." Apparently, Beveridge got tired of her antics and told Redpath to get rid of her. Flaherty said Redpath beat her badly, and she was immobile for several weeks. When somewhat recovered, she fled the den of iniquity.

Flaherty married a lumberman from northern Wisconsin in 1895, and that was when she came forth with a new version of the Beveridge murder. Based on her information, both Beveridge and Redpath were arrested and jailed in Ontonagon.

It did not bode well for the men; their futures looked bleak. Neither had led a faultless life, and it appeared that their nefarious behavior had finally caught up with them. But they had a redeemable side. Unfortunately, it took a catastrophe to bring it to light. While lodged in the Ontonagon jail, the

The Ontonagon jail (foreground) where Redpath and Beveridge were jailed and awaiting trial. The courthouse is in back of the jail. *Ontonagon County Historical Society.*

worst fire in the town's history occurred. The summer of 1896 was brutally dry, and by August, even nearby swamps were drying up. The Diamond Match Company had stacks of wood and mounds of sawdust everywhere, and with no rain and unbearably high temperatures, it was an inferno just waiting to happen.

Seventy-five-mile-an-hour winds fanned the sawmill's tinder-dry woodpiles. Soon, the entire village was consumed in flames, and terror engulfed the fleeing residents. The intense heat roasted apples on the trees. The fire's heat was felt a half mile away. After a few hours, the town was decimated; more than 344 village buildings had burned down. Ontonagon disappeared from the map.

The fire was a serious problem for Beveridge and Redpath. They were locked in jail—and the keys were gone! Sheriff Corbett was off to another part of the county with the cell keys. His wife was left in charge but at first was unaware that she did not have the keys. During the height of the inferno, Redpath's new girlfriend went to the jail on a rescue mission. She knew they were locked up and feared they would be prematurely cremated. Mrs. Corbett now realized that she did not have the cell keys and began a search for any extra keys. Fortuitously, another set was found, and Beveridge and Redpath were released.

Mrs. Corbett had other concerns after their release. She had to get her children and infirm mother to safety. But the street was thick with smoke and fire. Terrified and desperate, she was unsure what to do. At that moment, Redpath and Beveridge appeared. Redpath helped the children while Beveridge towed the elder Corbett to Pigeon Hill, an elevated area that provided a safe haven for the fleeing party. Neither man fled after his heroic act, and both men turned themselves in the following day. Their humanitarianism would serve them well as a mitigating circumstance when they went before a judge.

With the Ontonagon jail burned to the ground, Redpath and Beveridge were transferred to the Bessemer jail in Gogebic County. The trial for the murder of Molly Beveridge was held on February 23, 1897. Although Redpath was part of the cover-up plan, he was granted immunity to testify against Beveridge.

Judge Haire advised the jury that even though Flaherty, the primary prosecution witness, had a sordid history, her past questionable behavior was not to be considered when evaluating her testimony. Despite the judge's statements, her past might well have led the jury to be suspicious of her credibility.

On March 4, they concluded that Duncan Beveridge was not guilty, and he was set free. One man served five years in prison for a murder that he may not have committed, and one man was exonerated for a murder that he may have committed. The truth will never be known.

Heroes come along when you need them.

—*Ronald Steel*

6
MENACING DANIEL DUNN

Seney brothel and bar owner Daniel Dunn killed several men before Jim Harcourt took his life in a Trout Lake shootout.

The Wild West depicted in movies and dramatized in books had nothing on Seney, a small town in the middle of Michigan's Upper Peninsula. Seney in the 1880s and '90s was to have an influx of lumberjacks who raped the wilderness of vast stands of virgin white pine. Capricious loggers decimated more than a million acres of pristine forest. Loggers thought the abundant forests would yield precious timber ad infinitum. They were wrong. It took only twenty years to render the land naked. The three thousand lumberjacks who flooded the small community didn't care about how much timber was harvested. Whiskey, women and fisticuffs were their only concerns, and these they pursued with reckless zeal.

In the 1890s, Seney boasted twenty-one taverns, three brothels in town and two on the Fox River. The most opulent of the in-town brothels was the Grondin. Lawlessness was rampant, and violators were often ignored. The county court at Manistique was too far away to be involved in minor fracases; as a result, a local informal court was created. It was usually in the back of a bar, and it became the place where the judicial process played out. The highly illegal arrangement served the community of Seney for misdemeanor infractions. Petty crimes like larceny, drunk and disorderly conduct and indecent exposure were often the kinds of cases that were handled by barroom justice. Anything short of murder the locals felt they

The popular Grondin Hotel and bar in Seney was a competitor of Daniel Dunn's and the Harcourt brothers' saloons in the 1890s. *Superior View Studio.*

could handle. In this quasi-court, perpetrators frequently went unpunished or had lenient sentences. It was thought that the local entrepreneurs and others in power could easily manipulate the system to their advantage.

At a court convening, the judge was usually nominated by those in attendance or seated by self-proclamation. Juries were selected from bystanders, and the defendant frequently was his own lawyer. The prosecutor, like the judge and jury, was selected from those in attendance. After the prosecution presented evidence against the defendant, the jury would decide guilt or innocence (most often guilt), and the judge would determine the sentence. Often it was a fine. The court had no legal basis, but in spite of that, it did, at times, hold those who violated community standards accountable for their behavior and had some success in keeping crime from becoming too rampant.

Rape, however, was a more serious matter, and the Seney court dealt much more harshly with rapists. "Watering" was the rapist's punishment; it was humiliating and painful. The perpetrator was bound with rope and brought to the nearby Fox River. He was then forced to disrobe, and with the removal of each piece of clothing he was lashed with a stout switch. The lashing continued even after he was nude. Then he was driven across the river naked, receiving a lashing during his trek through the shallow water. When he reached the other side, he was left to find his own place of shelter and some clothes. He was banished from Seney. (Banishment has been used as a form of punishment since biblical times. The Jews felt social isolation was a justifiable retribution for violating community norms. To the Jews, there could be no worse punishment than being rejected by your peers and driven into the desert.)

One resident, Daniel Dunn, tested the limits of Seney's justice and moral standards. Seney was ripe for corruption, and Dunn thrived in iniquity. The bar and brothel owner was not a likeable man. He had thick eyelids and bushy eyebrows and looked more the part of respectable banker than nefarious criminal. The former Roscommon resident was a paradox: he never smoked, drank or cursed, yet he ran a saloon and whorehouse and contemptibly trod over anyone who stood in his way. Dunn left downstate Roscommon when a warrant was issued for his arrest. After leaving, he had an old man return to the village and burn down his brothel in order to collect the insurance. He paid his beguiled accomplice fifty dollars for successful arson. He took the insurance money and then borrowed more money from a Roscommon druggist and built a bordello in Seney.

Typical of Dunn, he borrowed money easily but was reluctant to pay it back.

The druggist appealed to Dunn many times for the money; Dunn never responded. Exasperated, the druggist threatened Dunn with a lawsuit, and then he went to Seney to force him to pay. When the druggist arrived, the wily Dunn told him that he had discovered bog ore on an island in the middle of the Seney swamp and that he would soon have enough money to pay him back. Dunn had indeed discovered some bog ore, but its ore content was not sufficient to interest any mining company. Dunn took the unsuspecting druggist to the site and proudly showed him the ore that he had earlier strewn on the small island. When the druggist bent over to sample the ore, Dunn unceremoniously shot him in the head, pushed his body into the bog and covered it with branches. Much later, remnants of the body would be found at the site. Dunn was never prosecuted for the murder.

Dunn's accomplice in the arson of his Roscommon whorehouse fared no better. He kept coming back to Dunn for more money. Dunn knew he would spend it on whiskey and that might loosen his tongue and make him brag about burning down the bordello. Dunn solved the collaborator problem like he solved the druggist problem—with a trip to the island in the swamp. When they arrived at the island, Dunn shot the old man in the back and briefly examined him to make sure he was dead. Without missing a beat, Dunn went back to Seney to retrieve a shovel, and he then returned to the bog. He dug a grave in the spongy sand and buried the trusting old man. These grisly murders fed the rumor mill in Seney, but again, Dunn was not prosecuted.

Murder continued to follow Daniel Dunn. Six Harcourt brothers owned another Seney bar; they were loyal to one another and a tough bunch. They never backed down from anyone, but they were also likeable and honest. They were rivals of Dunn in the Seney saloon business, and they detested their nasty competitor.

In June 1891, twenty-year-old Steve Harcourt went to Dunn's saloon, probably on a dare, and ordered a drink for himself and the other bar patrons. A furious Dunn said, "No God-damned Harcourt can drink in my saloon." Harcourt then derided Dunn, telling others in the bar about Dunn's lawlessness. After angry words were exchanged, Dunn picked up a whiskey bottle and smashed it over Harcourt's head. Not content to just smash his skull, Dunn retrieved a gun from under the bar and shot Harcourt in the face. Harcourt desperately tried to defend himself and pulled a gun out of his pocket that was wrapped in a red handkerchief. He managed to get off one errant shot that missed Dunn and ricocheted into a picture that was hanging at the back of bar.

Dunn fired a second shot at Harcourt, hitting him in the abdomen. A seriously wounded Harcourt staggered out of the barroom door and into the street, where his stunned eight-year-old nephew happened to be. The boy assisted his uncle to Harcourt's mother's house, where she, to no avail, picked glass out of his skull. Harcourt died within a few days.

After the gunfight, Dunn was arrested for manslaughter and brought to the Manistique court, where the judge dismissed the felony charges and declared Dunn's actions to be in self-defense. Dunn had a charmed life—four times he was brought to court on serious charges, and four times he got off scot-free. But his time was running out.

Dunn feared revenge by the Harcourt brothers—and for good reason; the brothers' loyalty to one another had no bounds. The brothers drew straws to see which one would exact revenge. Jim Harcourt drew the short straw. Dunn was evil, but not a fool, and was well aware of what the Harcourt brothers were up to. He packed his bag and fled to St. Ignace, where he had a keep-peace warrant issued on the Harcourt brothers. Essentially, this was a preventative procedure that would enable the law to clamp down on the Harcourt brothers before any violence occurred.

Main Street in Trout Lake in the 1890s. The town was at the junction of the South Shore and Soo Railroads and getting the reputation as a den of robbers and confidence men. *Superior View Studio.*

Sheriff Dennis Heffron journeyed to Seney, where he served the warrant papers to the uncontesting brothers. The brothers accompanied Heffron to Trout Lake, where the party would change trains and then head to Manistique, where the court hearing would be held. They arrived early at Trout Lake and went to the local tavern for refreshments during the layover. Little did the Harcourt brothers know that above the saloon on the second floor were Dunn and his wife. They were staying there as guests of bar owner Jack Nevins. Dunn was also waiting for the next train to Manistique. From the second floor, he saw the Harcourts enter the tavern. Without any fanfare, he stuffed a revolver in his shirt and went down to the bar.

In the tavern, Dunn pulled out his gun, but not fast enough. Jim Harcourt quickly reacted to Dunn and fired four quick shots into him, one striking Dunn in the heart. His body fell lifeless to the barroom floor, a fitting exit for a man who had led a violent life.

Harcourt turned himself over to the sheriff who was standing nearby. Trout Lake is in Chippewa County, and as a result, Harcourt's murder trial was held at Sault Ste. Marie. Half of Seney's population was in attendance. Most thought that Jim Harcourt deserved to have a bronze statue erected in the Seney village square for ridding the town of the scoundrel. The judge, however, did not see it that way, and he found Harcourt guilty and sentenced him to seven and a half years in Marquette's State Prison. Harcourt, when asked by the judge if he had anything to say, replied, "I'm sure that Dan will not kill any more of my brothers."

Jim Harcourt was a model prisoner and, through the efforts of James T. Hurst, a state representative, was pardoned by the governor after serving only three years. He returned to Schoolcraft County, greeted by a jubilant crowd. The respected and talented Harcourt embarked on a civic career where he was elected township supervisor, deputy sheriff and conservation officer. Eventually, with his wife and children, he moved to downstate Houghton Lake, where he operated a gravel pit until his death.

After the turn of the century, when the white pine forests were depleted and the loggers were just a footnote in history, Seney faded into near oblivion. The hot summer sun peeled paint off vacant and tired buildings as overgrown grass and weeds slowly consumed the once busy streets. Today, a yellow caution light blinks forlornly on Highway 28, and it's often the only sign of life in the now sleepy hamlet. Truck drivers in eighteen-wheelers and tourists in shiny sport utility vehicles streak through the village, unaware of its colorful and bawdy history.

The days of rowdy, rough-hewn loggers celebrating a weekend in the village are gone, and all that remains are the tales of what once was the peninsula's wildest settlement.

7
DEATH—WHEN THE SUN GOES DOWN

Gust Adams, a Nathan tavern owner, closed his bar and went off to bed—he never saw the sun rise the next day.

On October 1, 1903, after he had breakfast, Fred Golden went to the Nathan saloon. This was his normal morning routine. Nathan was a remote train station in the center of flat and relatively barren Menominee County in Michigan's Upper Peninsula. When Golden arrived at the bar, it was quiet, and the front door was locked, which was not unusual for the early morning hour. Golden went to the back door but fared no better; it, too, was locked. He knew that one of the two owners slept at the bar and thought it out of the ordinary that no one answered. Either Charles Erickson or Gust Adams, the bar co-owners, rotated evenings staying in the bedroom in the back of the bar. They feared being robbed at night. Golden was certain that one of the owners must be inside. Concerned, he sought the help of Gene Houte and Paul Brunette, nearby friends, who immediately went back to the bar with Golden. In addition, they notified Charles Adams, Gust's brother, to come to the bar. They rapped and again got no response. Now more concerned, they pried open a rear window.

Once in, they went to a door that led to the back bedroom. Golden pushed to open the resistant door, only to find that obstructing its movement was the bloody body of Gust Adams. Three empty booze bottles were corralled by his splayed legs, and at his side was a partially filled can of beer. Adams's right hand clutched a key, and paper remnants were strewn about the body.

Houte at first thought it was a suicide, but the stunned men quickly realized they had stumbled on a brutal murder. Moving the body away from the door they found Adams's crushed hat underneath him and his torso laced with three bullets. The trio unsuspectingly walked into the aftermath of a murder, one that would rock the small community and shred family bonds.

Nathan is a hamlet forty miles north of the city of Menominee. Upper Michigan's southernmost county. It's located on County Road G-18, ten miles west of Carney, which intersects with U.S. 41, a primary north–south corridor. A ribbon of small towns, none larger than a few hundred residents, stretches along the highway.

Today, the saloon, houses and train station that composed the town in 1903 are gone, and the only evidence that the town existed is in old, faded scrapbooks that have been passed on to surviving heirs.

At the turn of the century, lumbering was the major industry, and Menominee was the second most important lumber export city in the United States. The forests have long been depleted and were replaced by dairy herds that span the county. The milk and cheese byproducts are primary to the county's economy. Hay and potatoes are the only crops that are grown in the thin, poor-quality soil. It is not an impoverished area but one that can sustain a living for those who are willing to work unending days. Farmers find refuge in their isolated homes during the long, dark and cold winters, as howling winds sweep with authority through the comparatively flat landscape and temperatures submit the hardy residents to the bone-numbing chill of minus twenty degrees. In the summer, scorching heat will often soar into the nineties, sending beleaguered cows to seek the shade of the barn. In the fall, the rustling of leaves and ensembles of birds provide soft music on tranquil country days. No matter what the climate was like, life in the county at the turn of the century percolated along with leisurely regularity, which suited the residents just fine. It was a time when life was simple, sweet and, above all, more manageable—but all that was about to change.

After finding the body, Houte and Golden left the tavern and rushed a mile and half to Charles Erickson's home to tell him that his business partner was dead. Erickson, forty, was a well-built man with a pleasing disposition, and by all accounts, he was well liked in the community. He was told between 7:30 and 8:00 a.m. After hearing the news, an emotionless Erickson told them, "I will change my clothes and go to the saloon as soon as possible." At the time, Erickson did not know that Adams was murdered. Later, he said, "It was queer as he [Adams] looked healthy the night before and I thought he might have died of heart disease."

Gust Adams's saloon in Nathan, Michigan. Adams was murdered in the saloon's backroom. *John Stevens.*

While Erickson was changing on the second floor, nineteen-year-old Amanda Hammerberg, who was the sister of Gust Adams's wife and Erickson's sister-in-law, said that Erickson shouted down to her, "I am glad I was not there so they could accuse me of it." Hammerberg later told the police the same story. Erickson would deny he said this.

Golden wondered why it took Erickson an hour and a half to get to the bar and also noted that he was dressed in his "Sunday best." His late arrival and impeccable dress struck Golden as odd. Erickson looked at Gust's body and then went to the cash register and checked the contents of the till.

The early evening of September 30, 1903, was much like any other fall night in Nathan. A spread of fall colors usually illuminates the gentle terrain, but that night, rain-threatening clouds cast a pall over the land, dampening the woodland complexion. Winter gray was patiently awaiting its turn, but it would be a while yet. It was a quiet night in the village saloon. An occasional patron dropped in for a beer, but that was pretty much it. One stranger sauntered in, had a beer and then left. Huddled in the bar on that chilly night, playing smear and drinking beer, were Gust Adams, Fred Crane, Eugene Houte and Solomon Swanson. Adams was doing double duty that evening, both tending bar and playing cards. Bar traffic was light, and he could easily do both. Erickson dropped in at the bar at 8:30 p.m. and sat in for a hand of cards. He was on his way to the train station to pick up his wife, but he had an hour to kill before her 10:00 p.m. arrival. The train station was only four hundred feet from the tavern, a short jaunt for Erickson. He played a hand and, at 9:40 p.m., departed for the train station. With Erickson leaving, the card game broke up, and everyone except Adams left the bar; it was his last night to stay in the bedroom in the back.

The investigation into the Adams's murder at first seemed promising. There were several leads that mandated investigation. Even with that, Sheriff John Stiles had his work cut out; solving this case would take hard work. Stiles sought the assistance of Thomas Johnson, a Chicago Pinkerton detective. The Pinkertons were a private security guard agency founded in Chicago in 1850. The Pinkertons had a stellar reputation, and Stiles thought he could bring their considerable skill to solving the murder.

One encouraging lead was a memorandum book that Adams kept. A section of the book purportedly contained the names of people to whom Adams had lent money. This could have been significant if it were true. Adams's prosperity in the bar business enabled him to lend money to friends and neighbors. In effect, he was a de facto bank for the community. After Adams's murder, the police searched for the memorandum book that was usually on his person. However, it was missing and did not turn up until ten days after the murder, when Jennie Adams, Gust's wife, mysteriously found it in her dresser. When it did turn up, a bloody thumbprint was found on one of the pages. However, that bit of evidence went nowhere, and to whom the thumbprint belonged was never identified. In addition, several pages had been ripped out of the book, and what remained was of little use to the police.

Another lead the police had was a dog. Adams and Erickson had a bulldog that stayed in the bar at night. It was friendly to those it knew but barked ferociously when strangers approached. The dog was kept in the back entry and would have barked at an unknown intruder. The night Adams was murdered, no one in the vicinity heard the dog bark. The police theorized that whoever surreptitiously broke into the bar that evening knew the dog and that was why it failed to bark.

Suspecting that the murder may have been tied to a robbery, the police examined the crime scene for theft. It was well known that Adams always had money either on his person or in the bar. A search of the bedroom yielded a canvas bag of money under the mattress, and cash was still in the bar till. Reports varied on whether Adams had any cash on his person the night of the murder. Robbery did not appear to be a likely motive for the murder.

The investigation turned titillating when it was revealed that Gust Adams's brother, Charles, may have been having an affair with Gust's wife, Jennie.

A letter Charles Adams received from Jennie Adams after her husband was murdered was never disclosed in court. What it contained remained a mystery. Charles said Jennie told him to burn the letter after he read it. He said that the letter was not incriminating and that he turned it over to attorneys Doyle and Mills. Nothing significant came of the mystifying letter in the court proceedings.

In an attempt to get information to solve the crime, a $1,000 reward was offered for information leading to the capture and conviction of the murderer of Gust Adams.

Jennie Adams was not content to let the local police solve the murder; she solicited the services of a psychic from Chicago. This was not new for Jennie. She had long been a believer in mediums, and her employing one would not have been considered unusual. In one of her sessions, the medium said, "He is a large man who has committed the deed; broad shouldered, very dark complexioned, smooth face; one should judge about forty-five years of age with extremely large hands."

The police were not pleased with Jennie's seeking the services of a medium. Besides making them look incompetent, they felt that mediums were nothing more than charlatans attempting to extort money from a vulnerable, grieving widow. She was told it was best to leave spirits out of the case. So with this police encouragement, Jennie discontinued consulting the psychic. It was just as well, as the medium's efforts were of little use and did not bring a killer to justice.

After a ten-month investigation, and in a much-anticipated move by the prosecution, Charles Erickson was arrested at his home on August 18, 1904, and charged with the murder of his business partner. His children and wife, Christina, were home at the time of his arrest; they wept as he was led off to the Menominee County jail. According to visitors, he remained in good spirits during his incarceration.

On August 26, eight days after his arrest, a preliminary hearing was held in Menominee's circuit court to determine if there was sufficient evidence for Erickson to be bound over for trial. Prosecutor Charles Line prepared the case and turned it over to the new prosecutor, Charles F. Juttner, while attorneys Michael Doyle and Donald Mills defended Erickson. Martin Vandenberg was the sitting judge.

The court battle was waged over circumstantial evidence. The prosecution's case relied heavily on Erickson's demeanor during the early stages of the investigation and what, Line said, were self-incriminating comments. Line stated that Erickson had a "cold-blooded attitude" after the murder.

Charles Erickson (right) and Gust Adams (left) on the porch of the Nathan Saloon. *John Stevens.*

In addition, he cited the comment Erickson purportedly said to Amanda Hammerberg: "I am glad I was not there so they could blame me for it." And on the morning Erickson entered the bar where his business partner lay dead on the floor, Line said that Erickson was heard saying, "I must clear myself, I must clear myself." Line believed that Erickson's behavior and comments made him the murderer. The prosecutors did not have any direct evidence. Nor did they suggest what Erickson's motive might have been.

Johnson, the Pinkerton detective, was actively involved in the case. In a thinly veiled disguise as a fruit peddler, Johnson not-so-secretively sleuthed around the county conducting interviews with anyone who knew Erickson. Johnson said, "Erickson was the craftiest, shrewdest man he had ever been up against." The locals were impressed that a Pinkerton detective was involved in solving the murder. However, no matter how large a shadow he cast, the bombastic detective did little to solve the case. Flashes of silence would have made Johnson more bearable.

Defense attorneys Mills and Doyle said the state lacked the evidence to bring the case to trial. Doyle said, "We hear not a tittle of anything like evidence. His life has been of irreproachable character and reputation, a good citizen, faithful husband and father." In continuing the attack on the prosecution, Mills disparaged the Pinkerton detective hired by the state as nothing more than "a dime novel diamond dick detective." Doyle continued his attack, saying, "The newspaper accounts are atrociously unjust."

After hearing from both the prosecution and the defense, Judge Vandenberg ruled there was ample evidence for Erickson to be bound over for trial. Erickson shook his head in disbelief, while his petite wife held his hand and shed a spate of tears on hearing the court's ruling.

Erickson's bail was set at $10,000, an enormous sum at the turn of the century, but he had benefactors who rallied to his side during the dark days. Coming to his assistance with bail money were the Menominee River Brewing Company and Liesen & Henes Brewing Company. It was not considered out of the ordinary for the brewing companies to come to Erickson's assistance; he owned a bar and had long purchased beer from the breweries. What was unusual is that the court permitted bail on a charge of first-degree murder. Bail rarely happens on a murder charge. Apparently, Vandenberg did not see Erickson as a flight risk.

While out on bail, Charles Erickson became upset with what he said were slanderous statements Charles Hammerberg made that indicated Erickson was the one who murdered Adams. Erickson contended that Hammerberg, who was his father-in-law, as well as Adams's, made slanderous statements in front of Jenny Adams and his wife, Christina, in February 1904. Erickson was seeking $5,000 in damages from Hammerberg. Hammerberg vehemently denied making any slanderous comments to anyone about Erickson. It took a jury only a few minutes of deliberation to find Hammerberg not guilty. The slander lawsuit was peripheral to the ongoing murder investigation, but it was titillating and stoked the public's fascination with the murder.

On February 6, 1905, sixteen months after the murder of Gust Adams, the trial of accused murderer Charles Erickson began. The *Daily Eagle-Star*, a local paper, said it would be "the most sensational trial that has ever taken place in the county." The courtroom was packed, and the downstairs hallways were filled with people eager to gain entry in anticipation of hearing salacious testimony. The trial stimulated gossip, and its yearlong saga pitted family against family in the tightly knit community. Coffee shops and bars hummed with scuttlebutt as residents freely offered their opinions of who killed Gust Adams. The paper made much of the fact that both the murdered man and the alleged murderer married Charles Hammerberg's daughters.

The trial took place in the opulent and historic Menominee County courthouse, in the city of Menominee. Built in 1875, the "high Victorian Italianate" structure is typical of the grand courthouses built in the later part of the nineteenth century. With his life hanging in the balance, it is doubtful that Erickson paid much attention to the incredibly crafted architecture.

The trial was expected to last one week. The second day was devoted to selecting twelve jurors from the sixty who were summoned. It took three and a half hours to impanel the twelve who would make up an all-male jury. Interestingly, the trial took place eight years before the Nineteenth Amendment was enacted. This amendment provided women with political equality, including the right to be on juries. After the jury was selected, it was sequestered on the second floor of the courthouse, where the jurors read, smoked and played cards until they retired for the night on cots provided by the court.

The prosecution's case rested largely on Erickson's statements that were heard at the preliminary hearing. Martha Krueger, a young house domestic in the Erickson home, testified at the time that she overheard the conversation between Amanda Hammerberg and Erickson the morning of the murder and said she did not hear Erickson make any self-incriminating statements.

The prosecution said that Erickson told Charles Hammerberg, "The business will be better now. I'll spend every cent I have to clear myself." Prosecutor Line said Erickson was nervous after the murder. Line continued that Erickson did not express any excitement when told of his partner's death.

A major witness for the prosecution was Johnson, the Chicago Pinkerton, who was expected to have damning evidence against Erickson. On the stand, Johnson did not have any stunning revelations that would be detrimental to the defendant. Under cross-examination by Mills, Johnson said at one time he suspected both Fred Golden and Charles Hammerberg of the murder. In spite of not offering any valuable information about the crime, the county paid him $275 for his fruitless efforts. In a stellar defense move, Mills capitalized on Johnson's testimony and made it appear that either Golden or Hammerberg should be on trial.

Many of the witnesses who testified said that Erickson was not a quarrelsome man and that he and Gust Adams had a cordial relationship.

The prosecution made much of the key clutched in Adams's hand when he was found dead. Testimony over the key was confusing. The prosecution attempted to identify the key with Erickson and his knowledge of how the bar door locks worked. The key testimony, however, seemed only to obfuscate rather than bring clarity to solving the murder.

On February 10, 1905, the jury rendered a verdict—not guilty. It took only ten minutes to come to a conclusion, a very short time by any standard. It was not much of a surprise to the residents in the county; many felt there was little evidence to convict Erickson.

Erickson responded to the jury's decision, saying, "I felt safe all the time, for how could they convict an innocent man?" Immediately after the rendering of the verdict, supporters rallied around Erickson in the courtroom, offering their congratulations.

Christina Erickson was steadfast in support of her husband throughout the trial. When the couple exited the courthouse, a friend across the street yelled out his congratulations; the jubilant couple beamed with satisfaction.

The trial was not cheap for Erickson; he spent $2,000 to defend himself. In today's money, that would be $40,000. It was no bargain for the state either, costing the county prosecutor's office $4,000.

If not Erickson, then who killed Gust Adams? After the trial, defense attorney Mills stated unequivocally that others were more likely to have killed Adams than his client Charles Erickson. Mills said a case could have been made against Charles Adams. The alleged affair that Charles Adams had with his brother's wife made him a prime suspect. Mills cited the clandestine letter that Charles had received from Jenny Adams as a powerful motivation for murder.

Mills said bad blood existed between Charles Erickson and Charles Hammerberg and that Hammerberg's involvement also raised unanswered questions. Could he have been responsible?

Or did the shadowy stranger who wandered into the bar that fateful night have something to do with Gust Adams's departure?

Prosecuting attorney Line, for whatever reason, did not indict anyone else for the murder and it remained unsolved.

On Sunday, January 27, 1941, thirty-six years after his exoneration, Charles Erickson died; he was seventy-seven. He was survived by his wife and seven children. After a funeral service in Erickson's home, he was buried in the Nadeau Township Cemetery. He went peacefully to his grave knowing that his neighbors and friends stood by him during the dark days over three decades earlier. They believed in his innocence and were steadfast in their support.

Thus, the final chapter of Gust Adams's murder was laid to rest, but for several years after the murder, it continued to be the talk of the town. Today, the memory of what happened over one hundred years earlier has faded, and few residents are familiar with the intriguing tale of Gust Adams.

Perhaps Woody Allen said it best about what Erickson may have felt during his trial for murder: "This trial is a travesty; it is a travesty of a mockery of a sham of a mockery of travesty of two mockeries of a sham. I move for a mistrial."

The saloon and the train station are gone, and time moves slowly in Nathan. Nothing is left to trigger the imagination of what happened so long ago; it will remain forever a secret.

The $1,000 reward remains uncollected.

8

A DEADLY AMBUSH

Three slain in a Painesdale boardinghouse in the midst of the 1913 Keweenaw copper strike.

It was December 7, 1913, two o'clock in the morning on a typical cold, blustery winter night in Painesdale, a small, Upper Peninsula mining community located just south of Houghton. Mrs. Dally had prepared tea for a late-arriving boarder and then retired to read quietly in a room that once was a parlor. Her husband, Thomas Dally, slept quietly in an adjacent bedroom. The Dallys ran a boardinghouse for English immigrant miners who labored in the Calumet copper mines. It was a "double house" in that it had an attached but separate house. The Dallys occupied half of the house located near the woods at the end of Baltic Street in the miners' village, and five boarders occupied the other half, while in the attached dwelling lived the Adna Nicholson family. The Nicholsons had five children who ranged in age from three to sixteen. Nothing was out of the ordinary on that cold December evening, and Christmas was just around the corner. The holiday spirit was in the air.

Out of nowhere, a cacophony shattered the stillness as an avalanche of soft-shelled .30-30 bullets penetrated the wood-framed boardinghouse, piercing the thin walls and sending lethal splinters in all directions. Thomas Dally, sleeping contentedly in his bed, was slammed with a .30-30 bullet that ripped into his skull. His wife rushed to the bedroom only to find her husband seriously wounded. He looked pathetically at his wife and said,

Horse-drawn hearses travel down Sheldon Avenue in Houghton during the Jane/Dally funeral procession. *Michigan Technological University Archives.*

"Can't you do something for me?" But the wound was mortal, and he died. Frightened and grief stricken, Mrs. Dally wept as she watched life slowly ebb from her husband's body.

On the second floor, the Jane brothers, Arthur and James, lay sleeping when one of the bullets tore through Arthur's head and continued its deadly journey, striking James, who was beside him. They were killed instantly.

A barrage of bullets also penetrated the Nicholson household. Two bullets hit thirteen-year-old Mary Nicholson; one grazed her head while the other inflicted a more serious wound in her shoulder. Two other Nicholson children, Marcia (sixteen) and Rozanne (eleven), although not physically injured, narrowly escaped death when bullets passed through the pillows they were sleeping on.

The Jane brothers, both in their twenties and in the prime of their lives, had just returned from Canada the day before and were eagerly anticipating returning to work in one of the copper mines that was still operating, despite a large, regional union strike.

Earlier that evening, they and a dozen immigrant miners had been in a festive spirit, singing Christmas carols and planning to attend morning worship services at the Methodist Episcopal Church. It was a good time for the brothers, who were pleased they could finally leave Canada and return to their home in the Copper Country.

Why was there a lethal assault in the middle of the night on the Nicholson and Dally homes? It turned out that the Dally house was known to have "scab" laborers, miners who were willing to cross the union picket line and continue to work. The Western Federation of Miners (WFM) considered the Jane brothers scabs.

John Huhta, Nick Verbanac, Hjalimer Jallonen and John Juuntunen were responsible for the killings and were active members of the WFM. Verbanac, an Austrian, and Huhta, a Finn, were friends for some period of time and, at one time, roommates. Huhta was the local WFM secretary, earning $75 a month, while Verbanac was a union organizer and made $125 a month. These were considered decent jobs, and the pay was commensurate with working full time in the mine and a lot less backbreaking than toiling underground ten hours a day. They were angry with those who supported the mining companies by going back to work. For the most part, it was the English immigrant miners (Cousin Jacks) who wanted to work, regardless of the strike. The English were more experienced miners in that many had worked the coal mines in their homeland of Cornwall, England. In the Copper Country mines, the English had the better jobs; they were the captains and shift managers. The Dally household had five English immigrant residents, making it an easy mark for the angry unionists.

John Huhta (second from left), confessed killer of the Jane brothers, marches with members of the Western Federation of Miners during the 1913 copper miners' strike. *Michigan Technological University Archives.*

That infamous evening, the four plotters armed with .30-30 rifles walked three miles to the Dally house and stealthily concealed themselves in the woods not more than fifty yards away. In the early morning hours, they rested their weapons on tree branches, took aim and unleashed a volley of bullets into the house.

The mining community was outraged at this turn of events. They blamed the WFM for putting Huhta and his cohorts up to the killings. The locals felt that the union was controlled by outside agitators, primarily socialists and communists who created an "assassin squad." In addition, it pitted ethnic group against ethnic group. Animosity among English, Slavs and Finns was already a problem, and the killings exacerbated an already potentially explosive condition.

Huhta's murder trial was held in Marquette in 1914, some nine months after the killings. The judge charged the jury to not only decide Huhta's guilt or innocence but also determine if there was a conspiracy by the WFM in the murders. Huhta, who had confessed to the murders, pleaded innocent at his trial. His lawyers contended that his companions had talked him into

The Dally home shortly after the ambush. The white marks on the house indicate bullet entry locations. *Michigan Technological University Archives.*

confessing so they could collect reward money. In addition, Huhta's lawyers maintained that he was intoxicated at the time of his confession and had been so for several weeks. Several months after his arrest, Huhta spoke ill of the union; he felt that he had been duped and blamed it for the mess he was in. Regardless of the defense's arguments, the jury, in only thirty-eight minutes of deliberation, found Huhta guilty of murder in the first degree and sentenced him to life in prison.

Huhta died from tuberculosis at Marquette Branch Prison in November 1918. At the time of his death, he had been incarcerated for four years; he was only twenty-eight. Ironically, his sentence had been commutated, and he was scheduled to be released in November 1924.

Murder charges against Verbanac, Jallonen and Juuntunen were dismissed, as were the conspiracy charges against the WFM.

Most of the upheaval during the 1913–14 copper strike was between labor and management. The WFM was locked in a death struggle with the mining companies, Calumet & Hecla and the Copper Range Company. The Jane/Dally murders, however, were not the result of labor versus management but of a division in the labor union itself. There were those who aligned

Michigan's National Guard (125th Infantry) was called in to keep peace during the 1913 strike. The troops (2,500) encamped throughout the mining community, including at churchyards and schools. *Michigan Technological University Archives.*

themselves with the WFM and honored the strike, while others felt that working to support their families was a higher calling.

The Jane/Dally murders clearly pointed out that in addition to miners having differing views on the strike, ethnic differences contributed to the conflict. The English did not consider themselves immigrants but extensions of the indigenous English population that had colonized America. They were the skilled workers with better jobs in the mines and were considered elitists, while the Croatians, Slovenians and Serbs had the more menial jobs and were relegated to a lesser position in the informal caste system.

Like it or not, there was an ethnic class caste system that was fundamental to the Copper Country's social structure. The Jane/Dally murders were more than just a struggle of workers pitted against management but also an ethnic struggle that set mining brother against mining brother.

In the early 1820s, when Henry Schoolcraft found copper in the Keweenaw Peninsula, he likely never dreamt of how that rich ore body ninety years later would become the site of an embittered strike that spewed blood on the Keweenaw landscape.

9

A STAIRCASE TO DEATH

Italian Hall Disaster

Seventy-three die in Calumet's Italian Hall during the infamous copper mining strike in 1913.

Five hundred children gaily pranced about, their eyes dancing with delight and reflecting a rainbow of colors from the lights on a nearby Christmas tree. The children on the second floor of the Italian Hall eagerly pressed forward toward the stage at one end of the room in anticipation of a gift from Santa, who was positioned prominently at the front of the stage. It was a snowy Christmas Eve in 1913 in Red Jacket, a thriving copper-mining town in the Keweenaw Peninsula that was renamed Calumet. For the children, this was the best of times.

Then, the unbelievable happened.

Someone yelled, "Fire!"

Panic was rampant in the Italian Hall as the alarmed adults and children quickly scurried to an exit that led down a staircase to the first floor. Those who first reached the staircase bottom exited with ease; however, after the first few had escaped, the doors swung shut. The surging throng of Christmas merry-makers were pushed together at the bottom of the staircase with nowhere to go. In the ensuing mêlèe, the terrified victims became stacked like cordwood—one on top of the other. The only sound was the crying and weeping of dying children. The pile of bodies on the stairs was six feet high and extended thirty feet. Seventy-three people died there, sixty-two of them children.

The Italian Hall the day after the disaster in 1913. Note the half-mast flag on the top of the building. *Michigan Technological University Archives.*

What caused the congestion in the staircase? No one knows for sure, but two theories have been put forth. The most accepted theory is that the doors at the bottom of the staircase turned in and could not be opened when a mass of people was pushed against them. The second theory is that someone had fallen on the staircase and those who followed tripped over the downed body and were unable to get up.

There were three sets of doors at the bottom of the staircase: one immediately at the bottom, one that exited out of the building onto the street and one that led into Vairo's Saloon on the first floor. While it has been long believed that the first set of doors opened in, subsequent analysis of the doors has not supported that position. Photographs indicate that both sets of exiting doors opened out. The space at the bottom of the staircase only permitted the doors to swing out.

Regardless, this evidence is not widely accepted. A plaque at the site of where the Italian Hall once stood is dedicated to those who lost their lives. The memorial inscription declares that the tragedy partially occurred by inward-opening doors. The incorrect plaque placed at the site by the State of Michigan was corrected in 2013.

Dominic Vairo, owner of the saloon on the first floor, rushed to the second floor when he realized what was happening. He assisted as best he could during the pandemonium taking place above his tavern. When he returned to his tavern, he found that the till had been emptied and liquor stolen.

That Christmas Eve, there were close to seven hundred miners, miners' wives and their children on the second floor of the brick building. It was an ethnic mixture of Finns, English and Italians. Multiple languages provided the backdrop for the yuletide music that filled the evening air. A requirement to enter the Christmas celebration was union membership. Those attending had to show a Western Federation of Miners (WFM) membership card.

The gathering that evening was supposed to be a joyous celebration in the otherwise bleak and impoverished world of the local miners. Six-foot, two-inch strike leader Annie Clemenc had gathered fifty-eight dollars from local merchants to buy stockings, toys and candy for the children who attended the Christmas Eve festivities. Though it wasn't much, these were hard times, and it did provide some delight for the children.

It is remarkable that more people didn't die when one looks at the number of people on the second floor. Many were aware of a fire ladder attached to the side of the building, and hundreds scurried down the escape ladder, while still others jumped out windows to the roof of an adjacent building.

The catastrophe was for naught—there wasn't any fire. No one knows for sure who falsely yelled fire, but blame was placed on "strike breakers." The miners had been on strike for five months, and there was no end to the walkout in sight. They felt the tragedy was the result of the mining company's attempt to disrupt their Christmas Eve.

Several witnesses that evening said they saw a man wearing a dark coat with a cap pulled down and wearing a Citizens' Alliance button and that he was the one who yelled fire. The Citizens' Alliance was a group of local businessmen and community leaders who sought to be strike arbitrators, in

With chairs lying on their sides, the Italian Hall as it appeared the morning after the worst calamity in Upper Peninsula history. *Michigan Technological University Archives.*

hopes that they could settle the strike—so they said. The alliance purported to be neutral, but most knew they were aligned with management. No one knows who the man with the alliance button was—he just disappeared. Even though he was wearing an alliance button, it could have been a ploy used by anyone who wanted to disrupt the union's Christmas party and blame it on the alliance.

One thing is for certain: the responsible person was never found.

The aftermath of the catastrophe sent shock waves not only throughout the Copper Country but also throughout the nation. The bodies were taken to a temporary morgue. Someone noticed a hand move on one of the children. Resuscitation was immediately initiated, and miraculously, the child recovered. It is one of the few positive stories in an otherwise heartbreaking tragedy.

Most funerals and burials took place on December 28. Six churches in the community were at capacity for the funerals. Children's white caskets

Flower-draped white children's caskets at a church service after the Italian Hall disaster. Sixty-two children died in the cataclysm. *Michigan Technological University Archives.*

were in short supply, and many had to be obtained from churches in nearby communities.

The burial of sixty-two children, most in Calumet's Lakeview Cemetery, broke even the most hardened man. So immense was the task that it took one hundred miners to dig the graves. Men who used their shovels to extract copper from the earth were now digging graves to bury their children. Horse-drawn hearses transported the coffins to the cemetery. The sight of sixty-two white coffins headed toward the graveyard, each one shouldered by four men, was more than most could bear. The two-mile-long funeral procession was paved with tears.

The Western Miners Federation (WMF) felt the person who yelled fire knew what he was doing, knowing full well it could have resulted in the loss of human life. It is also possible that whoever yelled fire did so as a harmless prank, never anticipating the deadly disaster. We will never know.

The strike was finally settled on Easter Sunday 1914, some four months after the Italian Hall disaster. By then, it was too late for many of the

Above: Families, friends and miners gather at the grave site of those who died in the Italian Hall disaster. *Michigan Technological University Archives.*

Left: The doorway arch is all that remains of the Italian Hall. A memorial plaque behind the arch recalls the tragedy. *Author's collection.*

hardworking miners, who had left the Copper Country by the thousands for Henry Ford's burgeoning car factories in Detroit. They were not only making two dollars an hour more at Ford's, but they were also leaving behind the sickening memories of that fateful Christmas Eve.

Famed folk singer and left-wing activist Woody Guthrie wrote a song about the disaster called "The 1913 Massacre." Not all were partial to the song; many believed it was inaccurate and only designed to create class warfare—the rich against the poor. Guthrie's emotional and inaccurate lyrics said the miners were making $1.00 a day, but that was not true; they were making $2.50 a day. He cites that thugs were the ones who yelled fire and relished the aftermath, yet there is no documentation to support either of Guthrie's positions. But the song did serve Guthrie's agenda of depicting copper laborers as nothing more than chattel who were subjected to the whims of greedy and inhumane mine owners.

Christmas 1913 will long be remembered as the time the rugged Keweenaw wept.

10

SLAUGHTER IN SEEBERVILLE

Two Striking Miners Murdered

Two striking miners are slain in a Seeberville boardinghouse during the bitter 1913 Keweenaw copper strike.

The history of labor strikes in the United States is replete with bloodshed and violence, and the Upper Peninsula was no exception to the carnage created by the rift between labor and management. One of the most bitter and deadly strikes was the great copper strike of 1913–14. Fifteen thousand miners labored in the copper mines. They went on strike to secure better wages and safer working conditions. Although the strike is long past, the residents of the Keweenaw Peninsula still remember the catastrophic strike over the rich copper veins that lasted nearly a year.

Thousands of European immigrants were lured to the copper-laden land with the promise of jobs in the underground mines. In the latter half of the twentieth century, Croatians, Poles, Czechs, Slavs, Finns and English flooded a sixty-mile stretch from Delaware to Painesdale in the hope of making a better life. Often the miners' meager wages were sent back to their homelands to remaining family members to secure passage to the United States.

Copper mining began in earnest in the peninsula in 1848 but was discovered earlier in the 1820s by Henry Schoolcraft and geologist Douglass Houghton. By the turn of the century, mining companies employed thousands who toiled underground in harsh working conditions. In the bleak winter months, the dank caverns were home for immigrant miners; daylight

The house in Seeberville (now Painesdale) where Steven Putrich and Alois (Louis) Tijan were murdered during the 1913 copper strike. *Michigan Technological University Archives.*

was a rare and precious commodity that miners saw little of. Death lurked around every corner in the subterranean shafts.

Poverty-level incomes forced families to live in cramped conditions in company housing, while single men were herded into ethnic boardinghouses. Miners were aware of the huge profits that the corporations were reaping from their backbreaking labor, and they wanted a larger piece of the pie, something they felt the mine proprietors owed them and could easily afford. Recalcitrant mine owners were adamant: there would be no negotiations with any labor union over wages and working conditions. A precipitous chasm between labor and management grew larger—something had to give.

The day of reckoning came on July 23, 1913. On that day, renegade miners, without approval from their union, the Western Federation of Miners (WFM), went on strike. They were disgruntled with their paltry $2.50-a-day wage and long ten- to eleven-hour workday, but mostly they wanted the deadly "widow maker" to continue to be a two-man operation. The widow maker was a copper-extraction tool that mining company officials converted to a one-man operation. The miners felt that a one-man operation would not only be dangerous but also reduce the number of miners needed to operate the mine. The name alone is telling and ominous. In addition, the miners wanted the recognition of the WFM. Calumet & Heckla, the owner of the mine, refused to acknowledge the strike because doing so would mean recognizing the union and legitimizing the strike, something it vowed it would never do.

An unlikely strike leader emerged during the crisis: six-foot, two-inch Anne Clemenc, a miner's wife and household servant. She led thousands of strikers in protest marches through the streets in Red Jacket (now Calumet). As with many strikes, arrests were common and violence inevitable.

Steven Putrich, a Croatian copper miner, was murdered by Waddell-Mahon security guards during the bitter copper strike. *Michigan Technological University Archives.*

But on August 14, 1913, things got worse—much worse—when the conflict turned deadly. Events took a grave turn when two Croatians, Alois (Louis) Tijan and Steve Putrich, were gunned down in a miners' boardinghouse in Seeberville by men from the sheriff's department and their hired security guards (miners called them strikebreakers and worse), the Waddell-Mahon men.

Earlier that day, ten strikers, with nothing more to do, had gathered in a Seeberville park and leisurely drank beer on the grass. They consumed twenty-four quarts of beer before they disbanded and headed back to their boardinghouse.

Miners John Kalan and John Stimac straggled behind the others and

Houghton County sheriff James A. Cruise hired Wadell-Mahon security guards to assist in maintaining the peace during the 1913 copper strike in the Keweenaw Peninsula. *Michigan Technological University Archives.*

decided to take a shortcut though mine property. In an anticipating sabotage, mine owners declared mine property off limits to the nonworking miners. Kalan and Stimac were told to stop by company guard Humphrey Quick. Not drunk, but perhaps a tad tight, they defied Quick's warning and continued on. In a parting shot, Kalan turned to Quick and said, "Lookout for yourself you son of a bitch, I fix you…I fix you for sure [*sic*]."

Quick told nearby Waddell-Mahon guard Thomas Raleigh what had just happened. Waddell-Mahon guards were private security guards hired by the sheriff's office to keep peace during the strike. The miners, however, viewed the Wadell-Mahon men as nothing but goons and strikebreakers. Earlier, Calumet & Heckla general manager James MacNaughton had rejected Waddell-Mahon guard service, believing that hiring private security guards would only heighten an already tense situation. MacNaughton felt the militia that was sent to Calumet could adequately keep the peace. But county sheriff Steve Cruise said he was understaffed and couldn't get local men to intervene in the strike. As a result, he felt he had no choice but to hire the Waddell-Mahon men. After speaking with Raleigh, Quick then alerted his supervisor, Edward Polkinghorne, who decided that they should pursue the trespassers and arrest them.

Quick, Raleigh, Polkinghorne and Harry James, along with other Waddell-Mahon men, went to the nearby boardinghouse to find and arrest Kalan and Stimac. Though no arrest warrant had been issued, this did not deter the determined party from pursuing the trespassers.

The armed guard party, now numbering six, was only five hundred feet from the mineshaft when it spotted Kalan. The boardinghouse, erected in 1902 as a temporary structure, was a rickety building that unbelievably housed seventeen people. Ten occupants were miners crammed into the second floor of the story-and-a-half house. It was wall-to-wall beds. Joseph Putrich and his wife, Antonia, headed the house. The Putrichs and their four children all slept in the same room at the front of the house. All of the occupants were Croatian.

The enforcement party yelled at Kalan that he was under arrest. Kalan responded by saying, "Me no go." Two of the arrest party grabbed Kalan and yelled, "Come with us you son of a bitch!" In an ensuing mêlée, the miners attempted to rescue Kalan, who was being beaten with a billy club by Thomas Raleigh. During the scuffle, someone threw a tenpin (bowling pin) that hit one of the sheriff's guards. The guard pulled out his pistol and fired, hitting Steve Putrich, a miner near the boardinghouse on the fringe of the turmoil. Alarmed, the other armed security guards dashed to the boardinghouse and, from all sides, randomly fired into the house through open windows and doors at the defenseless miners and their wives and children. The miners did not have any guns. Pandemonium broke loose inside, with everyone frantically scurrying for cover.

The firing continued until all ammunition was depleted. Alois Tijan was hit in the back while climbing a staircase and suffered a mortal wound. Putrich, who had been shot outside, died in the hospital the following day.

A number of investigations followed. From the start, each side pointed a finger at the other side as instigators of the fracas. The hired guards said they had a legitimate right to pursue the trespassers and that they were only doing their job, although it was not the trespassing duo that ended up being killed but two innocent bystanders. The guards claimed that the miners shot first and that they were just protecting themselves. Evidence, however, disputed that claim, as no weapons were found at the boardinghouse.

The funeral procession for Steven Putrich and Alois Tijan proceeding along Fifth Street in Calumet. *Michigan Technological University Archives.*

The miners felt the assault was unprovoked and brutal, particularly in light of an insignificant trespass. County prosecuting attorney Anthony Lucas said the Seeberville tragedy was "wanton murder." Joseph Cannot, a prominent union official, said, "Sheriff Cruise's hands dripped with blood." The emotional rhetoric polarized the factions even further and made attempts to end the strike more remote.

On August 16, Harry James and Edward Polkinghorne were arrested and charged with first-degree murder. At first, the four Waddell-Mahon men who were in on the shooting were nowhere to be found. They showed up a week later after failing to convince the prosecutor to reduce the charges. The six men were charged with second-degree murder and were released shortly after raising the $60,000 bail.

The trial for the accused men took place on February 15, 1914. Three Waddell-Mahon men, Joshua Cooper, Arthur Davis and William Groff, were convicted of manslaughter (third-degree murder) and sentenced to seven to fifteen years in Marquette Branch Prison. Judge R.C. Flannigan recommended that the trio serve the minimum time. Polkinghorne received the stiffest penalty with a twelve-year minimum. Harry James was acquitted while Thomas Raleigh jumped bail and left the area.

The four convicted felons embarked for Marquette Branch Prison on February 17. Polkinghorne and his father openly wept as the prison-bound train departed the Houghton depot. This brought closure to the Seeberville murders, but the sordid event only further fueled the hostility between the immigrant miners and the mining companies. Peace was yet to come.

Alois Tijan's funeral was held in the Catholic Croatian church, St. John the Baptist, in Calumet. Five thousand mourners paid their last respects to the fallen miner. In a Croatian funeral custom, Tijan, a bachelor, was followed in the procession by ten women dressed in white, with one of the women marching directly behind the white casket dressed in a bridal veil. The women signified that Tijan's life ended unfinished. The impressive and heartfelt procession, accompanied by the Humu Finnish Band, solemnly wound through the streets of Red Jacket, with the men carrying boughs of evergreen and the women toting bouquets of flowers to the Lake View Cemetery. In a union gathering after the graveside ceremony, Joseph Cannon, a WFM official, stated that the tyranny of the mine owners was worse than the oppression that the Croatians had experienced in their native land from the Austro-Hungarian Empire.

When the strike ended on April 12, 1914, the miners had won some modest concessions, but not nearly what they wanted. Their union would not be recognized, and the infamous widow maker would continue to be a one-man operation. However, wages were increased fifty cents a day, and the workweek was shortened to forty hours.

Tijan and Putrich were unknown Croatian miners and small cogs in a contentious strike that shaped the Copper Country's history.

11

THE DANCE OF DEATH

A slit throat leaves a philanderer dead and mutes the gayety of a victory celebration.

The Anderson Boarding House (now the Kipling House) is located in Kipling, a sleepy hamlet near Big Bay de Noc, between Escanaba and Gladstone. It was named after famed British poet and novelist Rudyard Kipling. Superintendent of the rail line to Kipling—the St. Paul–Sault Ste. Marie Railroad (the Soo Line)—was Fred Underwood, who had the privilege of naming railroad stations on the train route. Underwood executed his prerogative by naming two towns after his favorite novelist. The other namesake, Rudyard, is located south of Sault Ste. Marie in eastern Upper Michigan.

Kipling was flattered that two towns in Upper Michigan were named after him and often referred to them as "My Sons in Michigan." It has been speculated that Kipling may have visited the two communities on his one journey to the United States, but there is not any historical evidence to support this claim.

As are many Upper Peninsula towns, Kipling's history is tied to iron ore mining. In 1891, when Cleveland Cliffs closed its smelting operation in Fayette, it opened another in Kipling in 1892. The Kipling site on Lake Michigan was geographically well suited for a smelter. Iron ore was transported from the Marquette range to the seventy charcoal kilns located at Kipling, where it was processed and shipped to points south.

With an influx of Cleveland Cliffs workers to the small but burgeoning community, it became apparent that there was a need for laborer housing.

The Kipling House, built in 1891, was the site of a grisly murder in 1918. It now caters to travelers as a bed-and-breakfast hotel. *Author's collection.*

To meet this demand, Erick Wallberg built a large boardinghouse and called it the Anderson Boarding House. John Anderson was appointed the innkeeper. It was one of six boardinghouses that were constructed during the smelting heydays. Of the six, only the Anderson Boarding House remains.

Many old boardinghouses were sources of sinister stories that have long since been forgotten, and the Anderson Boarding House was no exception.

In 1918, a scandalous murder occurred in the entryway on November 14. The murder was a headliner for months in the *Escanaba Morning Press* and the *Gladstone Delta Reporter*. It rocked the small community and riveted residents as they followed the tantalizing details of the vicious murder for the next two months.

John Malberg, a thirty-year-old boarder, was ruthlessly stabbed during a quarrel at the boardinghouse. Initially, it was thought that John Weina had killed Malberg. Just prior to the killing, Weina was thrown out of the house following a drunken brawl. When the police found Weina a short time later in another boardinghouse, he had a half-packed suitcase and blood on his shirt. He looked guilty as hell. He was arrested and jailed; the police were convinced they had their man.

Upon further investigation, however, it was discovered that Weina may not have committed the crime, but in fact, it may have been an enraged and jealous husband, John Anderson, who inserted the knife into Malberg's jugular. After viewing the evidence, county prosecutor T.E. Strom arrested John Anderson and charged him with first-degree murder. The first-degree murder charge was questionable; a second-degree charge seemed more appropriate. By all accounts, premeditation, the basis for first-degree murder, was not evident. If Anderson had killed Malberg, it was done spontaneously in a drunken rage and would be second-degree murder.

Malberg, Anderson and Weina had been drinking heavily on the day of the murder. There was considerable drinking that day. A war-weary country was celebrating the conclusion of World War I.

It was common knowledge that Malberg was attracted to the vivacious Ida Anderson. Apparently, John Anderson was not aware of this. During the celebration at the boardinghouse, Anderson encouraged his wife to dance and said to her, "Have a good time Ida, dance and be merry and my friend Malberg will dance with you. He will dance the old Finnish reels you love so well." Ida then danced with Malberg several times. According to the prosecution, liquor was doing its job on Anderson, and at some point, he became angry at Malberg for flirtatiously dancing with his wife. Strom maintained that after stewing for some time, Anderson, armed with a knife, attacked Malberg in the entryway of the house and slit his throat. Malberg lived for a short time before dying from a severed jugular.

The Anderson murder trial took place in January 1919, some two months after the murder. The prosecutor's primary witness was Erick

The Kipling House entryway is where John Anderson slit the throat of John Malberg in a drunken brawl. *Author's collection.*

Wallberg, who was on the staircase that looked directly into the entryway. He was also the only eyewitness, according to the prosecution. Wallberg said he saw Anderson stab Malberg in the entryway at 6:00 p.m. on the evening of November 14.

Wallberg's account of the murder differed considerably from Ida Anderson's. She protectively defended her husband and claimed that John Weina had murdered Malberg. She said she saw bloodied Weina stab her husband outside the boardinghouse. The outcome of the trial hinged on two distinctly different versions of how the murder occurred. The credibility of the witnesses would be vital in determining who killed Malberg. John Anderson said that Wallberg's testimony was unreliable and that Wallberg was unbalanced, mentally ill and not responsible for his statements on the stand. In addition, Anderson also said, "I was completely under the influence of liquor that evening and my brain was muddled."

The trial garnered much local interest; the courtroom was packed every day. It was the first murder in Delta County in four years, and area residents feasted on every word that was written about the case in the two local papers. It was the buzz in all the barber and beauty shops in Delta County.

John Anderson proclaimed his innocence right to the end. The jury, however, did not see it that way, and after two hours and twenty minutes of deliberation, it convicted Anderson of first-degree murder. Judge Huber sentenced Anderson to a life term at Marquette Branch Prison. Prior to the trial, Anderson was jailed and was described by guards as an exemplary prisoner.

Anderson sat emotionless at the announcement of his guilt.

Defense attorney N.C. Spencer said, "He did not seem to understand the full meaning of the verdict."

The fallout from the Malberg murder reached the Escanaba Dry Goods Emporium (allegedly a blind pig), which was formerly the Brewery Saloon. Frank Morrison, the proprietor of the emporium, was charged with the sale of seven quarts of liquor to the men who were partying at the boardinghouse. Morrison, aware that he was going to be arrested, left town.

Michigan was ahead of the national movement to ban liquor. In November 1916, two years ahead of the federal Prohibition law, Michigan passed an act forbidding the sale of alcohol. Ironically, in 1933, Michigan was the first state to approve the repeal of Prohibition (Volstead Act). County prosecutor Strom said the men who had purchased the whiskey for the boardinghouse party became "crazed with fire water." Two of the men served sixty-five days in jail for intoxication. In spite of Michigan law, drinking still flourished.

Those who partook were subject to arrest and jail time, but to many, it was well worth the risk.

Anderson spent his prison time only fifty miles away in Marquette. Ray Tackman, now deceased, was seven years old at the time of the trial. He recalled that when he was a teenager and on his way to Marquette, he saw a man walking down the highway near the prison who looked like John Anderson. He stopped and talked to him and found out that indeed it was. Curiously, at that time, trustee inmates could be released on occasion to enjoy a short stint of freedom on the outside. It was an honor system where the inmate was required to return to the prison after a brief respite from the sandstone castle. By all accounts, it worked successfully. It was a time when an honor system meant something. Michael Crowley, a retired warden from the Baraga Correctional Facility, said, "Things were a lot different then."

Ralph and Ann Miller bought the Anderson house in 1993 and spent three years and a small fortune converting the run-down building into an upscale bed-and-breakfast hotel. The restoration was remarkable. They made the guest home modern in comfort but old fashioned in spirit by intertwining old and new. The restoration maintained the soul of the house while converting it to a tasteful hotel. Charismatic Ann Miller made sure all guests heard the tantalizing murder tale; it added to the hotel's mystique.

The Millers sold the Kipling House in 2005 to Meghan and Robert Micheau. They bought a classic house rich in history.

12

"GYPSY BOB'S" REVENGE

In 1921, murderer and bank robber Robert Harper killed the warden and deputy warden at Marquette Branch Prison.

B old swatches of ink connected by intricate patterns of intertwining lines covered the body of slightly built Arthur "Gypsy Bob" Harper. His body was a sea of ink. It was said that he was the most tattooed man in all of Michigan's prisons. If he hadn't chosen a life of crime to make money, he could have easily earned a living working in a circus sideshow. Even his face was etched with a star on his forehead. At five foot seven and 147 pounds, he hardly looked like a hardened criminal—but he was. He murdered, robbed banks and took what he wanted. By the time he was nineteen, he was a hardcore criminal.

Ironically, Arthur Harper, a career bandit, was born in 1882 to a father who was a respected Philadelphia policeman. Not much is known about his mother's early life, but when Harper was a teenager, his mother was sent to prison for murdering an acquaintance. His criminal exploits made him legendary, even to the point of folklore. One of the tales was that Harper was born while his mother was in prison, though that is not true. Harper was a teenager when his mother was sent to do time. But the tale made for interesting reading, and many journalists published it without reservation.

After his mother was sent to prison, his highly regarded father was left to raise Arthur, but he had little luck in successfully bringing up the incorrigible boy.

"Gypsy" Bob Harper, the tattooed inmate at Marquette's Branch Prison, served seventeen consecutive years in solitary confinement. *Judith (Suvanto) Greene.*

When Harper was of military age, his dad convinced him to join the navy. Harper enlisted in the service but was kicked out for nonconformity and rejecting rules. Harper never listened to anyone.

The tattooed criminal with dark skin and jet-black hair received the moniker "Gypsy Bob" from his nomadic life. Although his home base was Detroit, he wandered around the country, committing crimes and plying his trade as a tattooist.

One of Gypsy Bob's early brushes with the law was in Binghamton, New York, in 1899; he was nineteen at the time. A series of house invasions with the homeowners being brutally beaten spread terror throughout the rural community. Gypsy Bob was arrested on suspicion of committing these crimes, but he was never proven guilty and was released.

The following year, he was arrested for nearly killing a grocer in a hold-up in St. Louis, Illinois. Harper was convicted and sent to a southern Illinois penitentiary, where he escaped and eluded capture for some time. By now, burglaries had become the staple of his crime life. For the most part, Harper was a loner; however, that all changed when he went to Detroit.

In 1918, Gypsy Bob assembled a group of five thugs in Detroit and began a succession of bank robberies. This crime escapade lasted close to a year before he was again apprehended and sent off to Jackson Prison.

Because of his lifestyle, Gypsy Bob had alienated his police officer father, G.W. Harper. While he was in Jackson Prison, his father wrote a letter to the warden that said, "As I am the father of Arthur Harper, I do not understand why you gentlemen show any mercy to such characters." Gypsy Bob's dad was clearly disgusted with his criminal son.

Harper even failed to get along with his disreputable friends. Roman Kubiak, a former member of Harper's gang and a fellow inmate, quarreled with Harper, and they became bitter enemies. Not to be outdone by attempting to kill each other in any conventional manner, they scheduled a duel to the death. Weapons of choice were not mentioned in the account, but unbelievably, this duel was to take place while the two were confined in prison. One day prior to the scheduled duel, however, Harper jumped Kubiak from behind in the mess line and fatally stabbed him. While dying, Kubiak called Harper a sneak and said, "The only way he could get me is from behind." With an already lengthy criminal history, Harper now had a prison murder rap added to his list of crimes. With that murder, Gypsy Bob sealed his fate: he would spend the remainder of his life in prison. After the Jackson incident, he was sent to Marquette Branch Prison, a remote penitentiary in Michigan's Upper Peninsula, where hard-core, nonredeemable felons are sent. He would spend the next thirty-four years there.

Amazingly, the volatile Harper adjusted without incident to his new Marquette prison home. Warden Russell put Harper in the outside trustee division where he had limited privileges. Not only was he a trustee and an exemplary prisoner, but he was also a role model for new, youthful offenders coming into prison. Harper frequently took neophyte inmates under his wing and unreservedly advised them to go straight; he was a beacon of hope to many young delinquents. He worked in the library and began a spiritual journey; he was frequently seen toting his Bible. It was hard to believe that recalcitrant and unrepentant Harper had turned over a new leaf, but he had—at least for the time being.

Harper's criminal life was not over. He had more fish to fry, and in so doing, he would enhance his already infamous reputation as one of Michigan's most dangerous felons—an image that he loved.

On December 11, 1921, Gypsy Bob Harper and two other inmates unleashed a reign of terror in Marquette's prison. Harper was upset with the new warden, T.B. Catlin. Catlin had taken away some privileges that Harper had been granted under Warden Russell. No one was going to take anything from Gypsy Bob, and Catlin was no exception.

Harper was determined to kill him and selected the movie theater as the place to do it. Unsuspecting of any trouble on a peaceful Sunday afternoon, Warden Catlin, along with Deputy Warden Menhennett, seated himself comfortably near the front of the theater, which previously was the

Three convicts: Gypsy Bob Harper (left) with fellow inmates Jasper Perry and Charles Roberts in the Marquette Branch Prison courtyard. *Superior View Studio.*

prison chapel. During the film, Harper moved quietly from the back of the theater to the front along the wall until he approached Catlin. Reaching his prey, Harper proceeded to stab Catlin and then attacked Menhennett, who attempted to intercede. Menhennett's son, a prison guard who was

Marquette Branch Prison warden T.B. Catlin died from a heart attack brought on by a deep knife wound he received from inmate "Gypsy Bob" Harper in a 1921 attack. *Judith (Suvanto) Greene.*

sitting nearby, also entered the fray only to be stabbed in his lung. Harper was joined by his two accomplices, Jasper Perry and Charles Roberts, who continued to knife the weaponless victims. As soon as other guards in attendance saw what was happening, they turned the lights on to see four hundred inmates scurrying about the theater. Catlin was seriously wounded but managed to escape the grasp of Harper. Charles Anderson, one of the guards on duty in the chapel, gave the warden his cane to fight of his attackers, but it was of little assistance against Gypsy Bob and his knife-wielding accomplices. Catlin then ran down a flight of stairs only to have Harper follow him. He grabbed a nearby blanket to ward of his attackers and then staggered into the deputy's office and barricaded himself by positioning his feet against the door. Prison guard Charles Muck was alerted to the mêlée and rushed into the deputy's office. He saw Catlin on the floor and his assailants at the door. Muck commanded Gypsy Bob and his cohorts to back off. Muck was joined by inmate Tofi Leon, who also had a gun. Harper, Perry and Roberts were herded by gunpoint into the west wing, where they were locked in. The pandemonium finally ceased.

Menhennett died the day after the attack. Initially, it was thought that Menhennett's wounds were not as serious as Catlin's, and he was sent home, where he died within twenty-four hours.

Catlin, who had been sent to the hospital, slowly recovered over the next month and began to assume some of his previous duties as warden. He appeared to be recuperating; however, his recovery was short-lived, and he died on January 26—forty-five days after the assault—from a heart attack. It was speculated that Catlin went back to work before he was fully recovered and that may have contributed to the cause of his heart attack. Catlin's death certificate stated that he died of a coronary occlusion. Harper became aware of the official cause of death and protested that he would be tried for a murder that really wasn't a murder. State authorities found a quick way to correct the problem—change the death certificate to "death by knife wounds." This was done, but it was all an exercise in futility. The state eventually ceased the prosecution of Harper, Roberts and Perry. It came to the conclusion that it wouldn't serve any purpose to prosecute men who were already serving life sentences. A trial would have been a waste of time and money. Some state officials cried for a state constitutional amendment to legalize capital punishment when one commits a second murder. But their outrage was dismissed, and Michigan continued its ban on capital punishment.

This was 1921, and retribution for inciting insurrection in a prison was severe. Harper, Perry and Roberts were subjected to flogging, a painful punishment designed to curtail any thoughts about causing more trouble. The prisoner was placed over a barrel, covered with a brine-soaked sheet and then whipped with a thick leather paddle. Harper and Perry each received thirty lashes while Roberts received twenty-five. Flogging could be shortened at any time by the prison physician if he felt it was warranted. Reports vary on how Harper withstood the flogging. One report said that he begged for the flogging to be stopped, while other reports said he endured the extreme punishment and did not crack. The latter seems more in keeping with Harper's persona.

Prison authorities allowed flogging of lifers who had nothing to lose by committing a crime in prison. It was the only way authorities felt that they could curb prison violence. Today's standards prevent flogging as "cruel and unusual punishment," and prison employees would be prosecuted for using this form of corporal punishment.

The worst of Harper's punishment was yet to come. He was put in solitary confinement or what was called the "bull pen." While in solitary confinement, Harper did not have contact with other prisoners and was allowed yard time only one hour a day. He served seventeen consecutive years in solitary confinement, the most time ever in a Michigan prison.

Catlin always denied Harper's allegations that he stripped him of his trustee status and, in fact, said he was overly indulgent to Harper by allowing him to raise canaries in his cell and to sell pictures of other inmates. Records are unclear about the truth of the matter.

Harper was returned to the general prison population in 1938 and served the remainder of his time uneventfully. In January 1953, Gypsy Bob Harper complained of chest pains and was sent to the prison hospital. He died of a coronary occlusion shortly after arriving. He was seventy-three. Gypsy Bob left a legacy of violence and bloodshed in his early years, but as he advanced in age inside the restrictive confines of a prison, he unobtrusively slid peacefully away—in an eight- by ten-foot cell.

13

A SATURDAY RUNNING RED

Deerton's Oscar Lampinen goes on a shooting rampage in Marquette in 1924, killing two police officers and one of their sons.

The 1920s was the era of flappers, bootleggers and mobsters, a time when insatiable appetites for pleasure and profit were quenched by violent men who wreaked havoc in the Windy City. Gangsters Al Capone, Dion O'Banion and Bugs Moran spewed blood in Chicago's alleys, side streets and warehouses and never gave it a second thought. It was a killing field where thugs, as well as cops, were struck down in Chicago's dark recesses, black holes that lurked with anguish and death during the racketeers' reign of terror. Bloodshed like this could never happen in a small town located on Lake Superior in Michigan's remote Upper Peninsula—or so the residents of Marquette thought.

But on August 23, 1924, that all changed. It was a quiet summer day, just like a hundred other days in the peaceful city, but death was in the air.

Before the day was over, two policemen and a policeman's son were gunned down, their bodies leaving a trail of blood between a Washington Street alley and a Harvey riverbank.

Patrolman Thomas Thornton had just finished his shift late Saturday afternoon. He picked up a *Mining Journal* to read in the alley behind Washington Street while he waited for his friend and fellow officer Walter Tippett to pick him up and give him a ride home.

Suddenly, all hell broke loose. Oscar Lampinen, who had just burgled Boucher's Drug Store on Washington Street, ran into the alley. Thornton,

Patrolman Thomas Thornton was found in bushes in front of the Harlow House on South Front Street after being shot by Au Train, Michigan resident Oscar Lampinen. *Author's collection.*

seeing Lampinen scurrying down the alley by Boucher's, was suspicious and ordered him to stop. Lampinen responded by shooting at the officer and running across the railroad tracks to Harlow Clark's front yard. Thornton pursued him and ran into a hail of bullets.

Tippett heard the commotion and ran to Thornton's aid. He found twenty-six-year-old Thornton lying in a clump of bushes, severely wounded. "Oh Tip, help me, help me; he shot me," said Thornton. Tippett asked if he knew who it was who shot him. Thornton said he didn't know, but he described him as a man about five feet, nine inches in a blue suit with a brown hat and weighing about 150 to 160 pounds.

Others had arrived at the scene by this time. Recognizing that Thornton was in critical condition, they loaded him into a car and took him to St. Mary's Hospital. Despite valiant efforts to save his life, he died from the gunshot wounds in the early hours of the morning. In his last moments, cradling his two small sons in his arms, Thornton told his friend, "I did my best, Tipp. That's all I could do."

Duluth, South Shore & Atlantic Railroad agent E.E. McIntosh, who assisted Tippett in getting Thornton to the hospital, ran over to the sheriff's office and notified Sheriff Johnson of the calamity. Johnson immediately contacted fifty-year-old Marquette police chief Martin Ford, who was at home. Ford's son, Lloyd, who had just graduated from high school and was planning on going to college to be a lawyer, asked if he could go with him. Lloyd was probably more excited about driving his dad's new Nash than he was about pursuing a criminal. Ford bought the car in hopes of fulfilling a lifelong dream of driving it to the Atlantic Ocean.

They first went to the hospital to see Tippett and then went over to Clark's yard to search for any evidence the criminal might have left behind. They found nothing. The Fords and Tippett then left to talk to the night turnkey at the jail. He reported that a man fitting the description given to Tippett had been seen walking down the South Shore railroad tracks toward Harvey.

The man they were pursuing was Oscar Lampinen, a twenty-year-old Deerton native, who was known as a crack shot and an expert in self-defense. Because of his skill with weapons and expertise in the martial arts, he was idolized by many of Marquette's teenage boys. A friend said that Lampinen liked to read cheap books on western adventures and Indian tales.

The Marquette City Police force in 1915. Martin Ford (top row, second from left) was the police chief in 1924 when he was killed by Oscar Lampinen. *Superior View Studio.*

A year before the shooting, Lampinen had enlisted in the army. Not suited for military service, he spent much of his time in the guardhouse and was soon drummed out of the service. When he returned to Deerton, he told friends, "Deerton is too small for me; I'm going to the cities." Lampinen wanted to head west to Duluth and then to the wheat fields in the north Midwest.

Arriving at Harvey, the pursuing party spotted Lampinen walking down a railroad track. They opened fire and chased him into the woods. Lampinen ducked down behind a riverbank and returned the fire. He hit both Chief Ford and his son, Lloyd. Lloyd managed to get off one shot before he was dropped. Tippett, searching a nearby swamp, heard the shots and came running. He rushed to Ford's aid but to no avail. Chief Ford gasped, "He got me, Tipp." Reluctantly, Tippett left Lloyd, who was severely wounded, to doggedly resume the chase.

Lampinen fired at Tippett, one bullet narrowly missing him and lodging in a tree near his head. Tippett then spotted Lampinen swimming across the Chocolay River. In the water, he was an easy target. Tippett fired, and Lampinen went down and then resurfaced. Tippett fired again. Lampinen sank and did not resurface. His body was later retrieved by the Coast Guard within twenty feet from where it went down.

Bloody Saturday was over. Two of the city's finest were dead. Marquette's thin blue line just became thinner.

The largest funeral in memory was held in St. Peter Cathedral for Martin Ford and Thomas Thornton. In a show of support, hundreds of cars formed a cortège that wound through town to the Holy Cross Cemetery.

Lloyd Ford tenuously clung to life in St. Mary's Hospital, which was only three blocks from the cathedral. Lying in his hospital bed, Lloyd heard the bells ring at St. Peter Cathedral. In a quiet but knowing voice, he said, "Is that for Dad?"

Lloyd Ford died the day after his father's wake. His funeral was held two days later. Stores were closed to honor the memory of the three men.

The *Mining Journal* established a $5,000 memorial fund for the families of Ford and Thornton. The largest single contributor was Louis Kaufman, who gave $1,000. In addition, the city authorized the pavilion concession stand at Presque Isle Park to be managed by Martin Ford's widow, Mary. It was the city's effort to financially assist the widow, who now had to raise two of her three children by herself. Ford left three surviving daughters: Lyda, twenty-five; Remona, eleven; and Eileen, five. Thornton left his wife and two small children: Edward, three, and one-year-old James.

The site on the Chocolay River where Oscar Lampinen was shot by officer Walter Tippett. *Author's collection.*

Eileen Kroken, age eighty-eight, is Martin Ford's last surviving child and lives in Marquette. Eileen said on the day her dad died, Marquette mayor Clark came to the house and told her mom about her dad's death. Eileen said, "I

Eileen Ford with a memorial plaque honoring her father, Martin Ford. It was given to her in 1992 by the National Policeman's Association. *Author's collection.*

remember running to my dad's car when it was driven to our home, hoping it wasn't true, there was a stranger in it—it wasn't my dad."

Although only five at the time of her father's death, Eileen vividly remembers his playful nature. On one occasion, he good-naturedly shaped the mashed potatoes on her plate in the form of a house. She said, "Later on in life, others told me that he was a 'witty Irishman.'"

Eileen said, "Mom took Dad's death real hard. She went to her bedroom and stayed there for a long time. She led a lonely life after he died. She never talked much about his death." Mary Ford never drove the new Nash; it remained in the garage for years collecting dust on its once shiny finish, never having the chance to spin down the highway in quest of distant shores.

The newspaper noted that a quiet service for Lampinen was held at his home in Deerton.

The Marquette City Commission went on record as favoring the state compensation law for families of police officers killed in the line of duty. Both the Ford and Thornton families would receive $4,200 over one hundred weeks under the state provisions.

Walter Tippett was unsettled after killing a man, justifiable as it was. He later worked at the prison and then went to work in Ishpeming's underground mines. He had several brothers who were working in the mines, and it seemed like a natural fit and a safe place where he did not have to worry about death being around the nearest corner. Providence, however, interceded. In a cruel twist of fate, Tippett was killed within hours of starting his first day at the mine on November 3, 1926. This occurred only two years after the bloody shootout in Marquette. Tippett died in the worst mining disaster in Michigan: a catastrophe at the Barnes-Hecker mineshaft that claimed fifty-two lives in 1926.

On May 5, 1990, Eileen Kroken received a plaque honoring her father, the late Martin Ford, in a ceremony at the Holy Cross Cemetery. Eileen said, "I was honored but really nervous about being in the public eye—I'm really quite shy." On that day, National Police Officer's Day, all slain police and conservation officers from the Upper Peninsula who have died in the line of duty were honored.

Eighty-five years have passed since that infamous day. Marquette has been relatively peaceful since then. There have been other murders over the years, but none of the magnitude that claimed the lives of two police officers and a young man. Relative tranquility has returned, and that's just fine for the citizens of the peaceful lakeshore city.

14

THE SENSELESS SLAYINGS

Two Marquette conservation officers were slain when a poacher was threatened with a citation.

Fall in Michigan's Upper Peninsula brings not only a collage of spectacular color but also a burst of activity by deer hunters as they prepare for opening day. To many Upper Peninsulans (Yoopers), hunting season rivals Christmas as the year's most sacred day. The hunting ritual breathes life into the peninsula before the winter snow blankets the earth. Fall is a confused season. It is not quite sure if it wants to wrap itself in the lingering warmth of summer or prepare the inhabitants for the bitter cold months that follow.

To game wardens Arvid Erickson and Emil Skoglund the weather didn't matter—gray and nasty or pleasantly brisk, they were busy doing what they usually did prior to the opening of hunting season: looking for violators.

On September 29, 1926, Erickson and Skoglund were on a routine patrol in the Sands Plains, a jack pine–covered area located between Gwinn and Marquette, when they found a salt lick. Salt licks are deer appetizers that are often used by hunters to lure deer. Attempting to snare a violator hunting before the season began, Erickson and Skoglund obscured themselves in a bush near the salt lick.

In a short time, Roy Nunn and Joseph Contois arrived at the site. The officers recognized Nunn; he was a habitual game violator. Erickson and Skoglund came out from their cover and surprised the two men. Nunn had a gun, but Contois was weaponless. It is illegal to carry a firearm in the woods just prior to hunting season without a permit. A surprised Nunn could not produce a permit. Erickson told Nunn that he was in violation and would be taken to Gwinn for arraignment. Erickson then directed Skoglund to drive his car to Gwinn and said that he and Nunn would follow in Nunn's car. When they approached Nunn's car, Nunn went to the back and pulled out a .22-caliber pistol. He ordered Erickson to put his hands up. Contois, seeing what was happening, panicked and quickly fled. While running away, he heard a gunshot. Contois did not look back or stop but continued to sprint home. Because of his abrupt exit, he didn't know what happened to Skoglund.

In 1926, World War I veteran and Marquette County game warden Arvid Erickson was shot in the back of the head while attempting to arrest game violator Roy Nunn. *Judith (Suvanto) Greene.*

Contois arrived home breathless at 7:00 p.m. and told his wife what had just happened. Perhaps fearing he would be in trouble, or not wanting to get his friend in trouble, Contois told no one else. He feared Erickson and Skoglund were dead.

Thirty-year-old Arvid Erickson was born in Finland but came to the United States when he was six years old. He knew danger only too well: twice he was wounded while in the military during World War I. Erickson was a family man with a wife and two children under the age of ten.

Erickson's partner, Emil Skoglund, was a thirty-year-old bachelor who resided in a camp south of Ishpeming owned by another game warden, Andrew Schmeltz. Skoglund loved the outdoors and only went to town when he had to.

The next day, October 1, when the officers failed to show up for work, there was concern in the department that something may have happened. When they were still missing the next day, authorities began one of the largest manhunts in Upper Peninsula history. Hundreds of volunteers,

Strawberry Lake on Sands Plains is located ten miles south of Marquette and not far from the murder site of conservation officers Emil Skoglund and Arvid Erickson. *Author's collection.*

including game wardens, trappers and area residents, took part in several massive searches for the missing game wardens. By now, it was feared they were dead.

On October 4, searchers found a significant amount of human blood on Sand's Road, not far from picturesque Strawberry Lake. Discovered close to the dry blood were two spent .22 shells. They were significant finds but still did not yield information as to the whereabouts of Erickson and Skoglund.

Little progress was made in the case even after the discovery of the blood and the shells. In an attempt to shake something loose, state conservation officials offered a $1,000 reward for information leading to the capture and conviction of a suspected killer(s). Marquette County matched the $1,000, which swelled the pot to $2,000, a tidy sum in the 1920s.

Was it the reward that enticed forty-five-year-old Joseph Contois to come forward with critical information, or was it because he had a feeling of civic responsibility? Mrs. Contois claimed neither. She asserted that she was the one who encouraged her husband to go to the police and tell what he knew about the murder(s). In any case, on October 13, nearly two weeks after the slaying, Contois went to the police with his incredible story.

Contois said that Nunn came to his house on the afternoon of September 29 and asked him to join him deer hunting. Contois, aware that it was not yet deer season, went with Nunn but did not take a gun. They proceeded to the site on the plains where the salt lick was located. When Erickson and Skoglund showed up, all hell broke loose, and Contois said he quickly fled the area.

It was discovered that after Contois left, within minutes, Nunn shot Erickson and then Skoglund when he came to assist Erickson. Both died instantly. Nunn now had a problem—what to do with the bodies. His first thought was to toss them into Pickerel Lake (now Harlow Lake), just fifteen minutes north of Marquette. Nunn, however, could not find a deep enough location on the small, shallow lake to effectively dispose of the bodies. He then opted to submerge them in Marquette's lower harbor. He tied brick anchors to the bodies and dumped them off a dock into the icy waters of Lake Superior and was confident they would not be found.

Nunn attempted to hide the murder by dumping the bodies off the ore dock in Marquette's Lower Harbor. *Author's collection.*

After Contois's remarkable revelations about the murders, the police immediately went to Nunn's gun repair shop in Marquette and arrested him. Although Contois did not witness the shootings, he placed Nunn at the site of the crime.

Nunn emphatically denied any involvement in the mystery of the missing game wardens. Even after numerous interrogations, he stuck to his story. He told police that he had encountered Erickson and Skoglund that morning near Strawberry Lake and that he did not have a gun permit with him, but he did have one at home. Nunn said he and the officers drove to Marquette, where he produced a gun permit that he had purchased earlier. A check of the records verified that Nunn did have a valid gun permit.

According to Nunn, after showing the officers his gun permit, they all went back to Sands Plains. Nunn claimed, "I left them. I don't know what happened later."

Nunn was a scurrilous character. He began his crime career at seventeen, when he was sent to prison for killing his uncle. He was sentenced to life for the murder but had served only seventeen years when Governor Woodbridge Ferris pardoned him from Marquette Branch Prison. Little did prison authorities know at the time that Nunn would chalk up two more killings before finally receiving a permanent life sentence.

After his release from prison, it didn't take Nunn long to again be in trouble. Within a year, he robbed a store in Gwinn and was sent back to prison, this time for one to fifteen years. He served five years on that sentence and again was turned loose. He remained a free man for the next six years—until he killed again.

In the murders of Skoglund and Erickson, the evidence against Nunn began to mount. The police had not only direct evidence provided by Contois's description of what happened but also circumstantial evidence of a screwdriver found in Nunn's car that belonged to Skoglund.

The police felt they had a solid case against Nunn and began to put the heat on. They took him to the site of the murders and produced a blood-soaked coat that belonged to Nunn. Detectives then began to intensively grill him about the murders. Under repeated pressure, Nunn cracked and confessed.

On December 7, Nunn pleaded not guilty to murder in Marquette County Court. Early in the trial, Nunn recanted his earlier confession. He said the only reason he had confessed was because the state police had tortured him. In an unsuspecting defensive move, Nunn said it was Contois who killed the officers. The jury didn't buy any of Nunn's desperate last-minute arguments.

After deliberating a little more than a half hour, it found Nunn guilty of first-degree murder. (Second degree probably would have been more appropriate.) With Nunn's previous criminal record, Judge Richard Flannigan wanted to make sure that Nunn stayed in prison for the rest of his life and sentenced him to a life of hard labor at Marquette Branch Prison.

These senseless killings of two conservation officers occurred over a suspected minor hunting infraction that would have resulted in no more than a fine. Struck down in the prime of their lives, the two thirty-year-old officers were doing what they loved—protecting the Upper Peninsula's precious natural resources.

Nunn had a permit at home—he killed for nothing.

15

BLOOD BATH IN THE BIG HOUSE

In 1931, six were killed in a botched escape from Marquette's prison on the bloodiest day in the prison's history.

A long line of cars stretched down Spruce Street on a gray Saturday morning. It was a sad occasion, and grieving mourners had gathered at the house of esteemed physician A. (Alfred) W. Hornbogen to pay their last respects. That afternoon, one of the longest funeral cortèges the city ever saw wove through the city to the Park Cemetery, where Dr. Hornbogen was laid to rest.

Hornbogen came to Marquette to practice medicine in 1899, and for thirty-two years, he faithfully served the medical needs of the citizens of the community. In addition, he provided medical services for Marquette's prisoners at no charge. His humanitarian efforts cost him his life. Marquette Branch Prison inmate Andrew Germano callously and gratuitously murdered Hornbogen in a botched prison escape on August 31, 1931. Hornbogen was not the only one to lose his life that day; five other lives were snuffed out on the bloodiest day in Marquette's prison's history.

On the last day of August, Dr. Hornbogen volunteered to fill in for vacationing physician Youngquist. The day started no differently than any other day that Hornbogen worked at the prison. Dr. A.W. Hornbogen and his brother, Dr. Dan Hornbogen, who was also a physician, planned on driving to the prison together, when at the last minute Dan received a phone call from a patient on Lake Street in need of immediate attention. Dan told A.W. to go without him and that he would join him at the prison after he treated a patient for a severe nosebleed. Dan went to Lake Street, packed his patient's nose and then proceeded to the prison, arriving there a short time after A.W. By the time Dan got there, A.W. had been murdered. Had Dan gone to the prison with his brother, he, too, may have been killed. As fate would have it, a nosebleed saved Dr. Dan Hornbogen's life.

Dr. A.W. Hornbogen was treating patients in the infirmary on a routine Thursday. In his waiting room were three inmates: Andrew "Tony" Germano, Martin Duver and Charles Rosbury, all former Detroit residents. Germano, who was serving thirty to thirty-

Dr. A.W. Hornbogen was slain in a botched 1931 escape from Marquette Branch Prison. He was sixty-five years old. *Judith (Suvanto) Greene.*

five years for armed robbery, complained of stomach pains. Hornbogen asked Germano to remove his shirt so he could begin the examination. But Germano had a revolver in his waistband under his shirt, and he had not anticipated that Hornbogen would ask him to strip. He knew that taking off his shirt would reveal the gun. Not knowing what else to do, Germano retrieved the gun and shot Hornbogen in the heart. He died almost instantly. The escape had just started, and already things were going awry. Killing Dr. Hornbogen was not part of the plan.

In the same room with Hornbogen and Germano were head inmate nurse Frank Oligschlager and inmate assistant Leo Bolger. Quickly responding to the situation, Oligschlager knocked the gun out of Germano's hand. Hearing the commotion inside, inmate Martin Duver, who was in the hall waiting room, rushed into the examining room. Duver also had a revolver and, without hesitation, shot Oligschlager in the stomach. Oligschlager hung on to life for the next sixteen hours, and then he, too, died. Within minutes, one man was dead and another dying—and the mêlèe had just begun.

Nurse Leo Bolger picked up a porcelain rod and swung it at Germano. Duver, recognizing how badly the situation was playing out, shot Bolger. He was wounded, but it was not a life-threatening injury.

It was the early stages of an escape, and things would only get worse. The three conspirators quickly left the medical facility and entered an open area between A Block and B Block. While leaving, they encountered Warden Corgan and Deputy Warden Newcombe near the prison barbershop. With guns blazing, the fleeing prisoners sent a hail of fire at the two wardens. With bullets ricocheting off prison bars, Corgan and Newcombe somehow managed to escape uninjured and retreated to the gunroom. Corgan sounded the prison riot alarm that was housed in the gunroom. Guards immediately encircled the prison, and all prisoners were directed to return to their cells. In sounding the alarm, Corgan was hopeful that whatever was occurring would not spread to the general prison population.

The desperate inmates continued a reign of terror in their escape attempt. They came to the hall master's office, where Deputy Warden Joe Cowling and his secretary were conducting the day's business. The terrorists fired into the office and wounded Cowling. The convicts then grabbed Lieutenant George Hurley, the prison fingerprint expert, from the office and held him hostage.

The gunmen, with hostage Hurley, advanced to the prison yard, where they took another hostage, guard Alonzo Hulett. With the two hostages ahead of them, the three inmates scurried across the yard. It was made clear to the hostages that any attempt to escape would mean their lives. Hurley knew once they reached the entry gate that the convicts could exit to freedom. With that in mind, Hurley made a break for it when they reached the corner of the greenhouse. A barrage of bullets pursued Hurley on his gambled escape. Miraculously, he didn't get hit and made it to safety. One of the rogue inmates put a revolver to Hulett's head and pulled the trigger, but the weapon misfired. (The gun misfired because the weapon had been stored in a gravy can—all the weapons the inmates had were smuggled into the prison earlier inside chicken and gravy cans.) The three convicts then futilely pursued Hurley, which gave Hulett a chance to escape.

The desperate threesome then entered the box factory; from there, they went into a three-story industrial building. Charles Arnez, the guard on duty in there, was taken hostage. They advanced to the third floor, which housed

The Marquette Branch Prison where the Hornbogen murder took place in 1921. *Superior View Studio.*

thirty inmates. Another guard, Charles Alvord, was also taken hostage. The inmates and their new hostages were encircled not only by the prison guards but also by the state police and the Marquette and Negaunee City Police. The police and the guards now rained down a volley of fire through the open windows into the industrial building. The two hostages were ordered to close the building's windows with a broom and then forced to barricade the doors with inmate cots. The convicts returned the fire whenever they could see a guard or police officer through one of the windows. Panic enveloped the entire third floor, and everyone scurried about looking for cover. Germano, the leader of the escape group, compelled guard Arnez to write and sign a note that demanded prison authorities provide an escape car to be driven by Warden Corgan. Corgan's reply was swift and certain: he emptied a salvo of tear gas into the building. Tear gas filled the room, and the escapees knew that their chance for freedom was now doomed. Germano and Rosbury decided the only way out was suicide. They had agreed on suicide if their escape failed, and that time was now at hand. Duver was reluctant to join them in suicide, but he finally consented to the "final solution."

Recalcitrant Duver, however, did not go easy. He wanted to kill Alvord prior to taking his own life. One of the bunked inmates, who was not part of the plot, prevailed on Duver not to kill Alvord because he had eight children. The pleading inmate was not sure how many children Alvord had, but he correctly guessed it would spare Alvord's life. Duver pulled back the revolver he had aimed at Alvord's head.

Rosbury was the first to take his life. He inserted a revolver into his mouth and then blew his brains out. Germano did the same. Duver, the last of the trio, expressed one regret just before he took his own life: that he had not killed Hurley when he had the chance. Five were now dead and the fracas was still not over.

Inmate Frank Hohfer, who was housed in E Block, had a weapon and was suspected to be a part of the escape group, but he was barred from going to sickbay with the other escapees because Warden Corgan wanted Hohfer kept away from Germano. He knew if those two were together that trouble would follow. Hohfer was in his cell when he heard three shots ring out and rightly suspected that the other three had taken their lives. When Hohfer saw guard Al Fingel in his block, he fired at him with a revolver he had hidden in his cell. Fingel returned the fire and wounded Hohfer in the leg. After the initial exchange of fire, Hohfer took his own life as his compatriots had done earlier. The blood bath was finally over, leaving strewn in its wake four dead inmates, one dead physician, one dead inmate nurse, one wounded inmate and one wounded deputy warden.

Revenge may have played a role in the escape. Several weeks before the blood bath, Edward Wiles, a close companion of Germano, went to the prison hospital with a severe heart problem. On his deathbed at the hospital, he said to an attendant, "If I die, my buddies will clean out this place." Wiles's friends didn't succeed in cleaning the place out, but they did succeed in leaving a bloody trail through the prison.

How the dangerous inmates got the four guns was at first a mystery. An extensive investigation by the police, however, determined that a tinsmith in Detroit was responsible for smuggling the weapons into the prison. The guns and ammunition were hidden in cans of ready-cooked chicken. The cans, with the weapons inside, weighed the same amount they would have weighed when filled with chicken. Eventually, several other inmates, along with the tinsmith, were indicted for transporting weapons into the prison. Those convicted of the gun smuggling were sentenced to from twenty to forty years.

Michigan governor William Brucker, recognizing the contribution that several inmates made in assisting the prison guards to quell the escapees, justifiably and posthumously commuted the sentence of Frank Oligschlager, while inmate Leo Bolger's sentence was commuted to immediate release pending employment. It was the only time that Brucker ever commuted prisoners' sentences during his tenure as governor.

Hornbogen not only enjoyed the admiration of the Marquette community but also was trusted and well respected by the prison inmates. Had the foursome not committed suicide, their lives in the prison would have been tenuous. Inmate Jim Burton, who was serving a double life sentence, remarked about the inmates' suicide, "They saved me the trouble." Such was the esteem that Hornbogen had among the eight hundred inmates who were housed in Michigan's toughest prison.

16

DYNAMITE DISASTER

Killer attempts to eradicate evidence of murdering a Marquette conservation officer by using seventy sticks of dynamite.

S hortly after midnight in a wooded sanctuary just north of Negaunee, a brilliant light flashed across the darkness. Accompanying the illumination was an explosion that shattered the night air. Then all was still.

One hour later, another, louder eruption cracked the quiet evening. Then all was still.

Within hours, a third and final burst occurred, accompanied by a flare of intense light that danced into the darkness. Then all was still.

It was October 20, 1936, and not far from where the explosions occurred, S.O. Hoff and two conservation officers from Marquette were huddled in a car waiting for the morning light to see if they could find missing conservation officer Andrew Schmeltz. Hoff was a good friend of Schmeltz.

Shortly after midnight, the threesome heard the first explosion. Alarmed, two of the conservation officers sped to Marquette for assistance, while Hoff manned the site from where they heard the explosion.

Hoff heard the next two explosions before the search party returned. When help arrived, it was the middle of the night and too dark to begin searching for Schmeltz or the cause of the blast. But when the sun pierced the early morning, the search began. The team slogged through tag alders and mud before coming across a grisly scene. Stunned, they entered what looked like a scene from World War I's trench warfare, where scarred land was pockmarked with water-filled craters. Near the craters, trees were draped with pieces of bloody flesh that dangled like grapes on a vine. Hoff and the others assumed that the defoliated landscape and earthen holes were created by the dynamite blasts.

Amid the carnage, they found Schmeltz's revolver and holster and nineteen illegal muskrat traps. Unbeknownst to the search party, they were being carefully watched through binoculars by a young man who had concealed himself in the thick underbrush.

The search for the killer began immediately, and several suspects were picked up but later dismissed. However, it did not take county prosecutor John D. Voelker and Sheriff Rudolph Franson long to identify a logical suspect in the case—Raymond Kivela. Kivela was a twenty-seven-year-old trapper who lived with his parents, not more than a half mile from the site of the murder. Kivela hardly looked like a criminal, much less a murderer. Slightly built at five feet, eight inches tall and weighing 155 pounds, the bespectacled and hunched Kivela would have gone unnoticed in a crowd.

When Kivela was arrested on October 23, he scoffed at the insinuation that he had murdered Schmeltz. After several interrogations, he continued to proclaim his innocence. But when State Trooper N.H. Modders searched the Kivela farmhouse, he found evidence that implicated Raymond as the murderer. In the attic of the home, Modders found a pair of overalls still damp with blood and with pieces of human flesh stuck to the fabric. Further examining the overalls, Modders found a receipt in a pocket for one hundred sticks of dynamite dated the same day as the murder. But there was one problem with the name on the dynamite receipt; it wasn't Kivela's. In an attempt to establish that the handwriting was Kivela's, the police asked him to write his name and the name that appeared on the receipt. That was it—his writing matched the one on the receipt. He knew he was trapped by the evidence and confessed to the murder.

There was a mountain of evidence that Kivela had committed the murder. In addition to his confession and the bloody overalls, the dynamite at the scene of the killing matched the dynamite that was found in his home. Fingernail parings and paraffin casts taken from Kivela clearly showed that he had recent contact with nitrates.

The slain officer, forty-five-year-old Schmeltz, was a lifelong Yooper. Born and raised in Ishpeming, he loved the outdoors and was well suited to be a trapper for Michigan's Department of Conservation. He was a dedicated guardian of the wilderness. The veteran of World War I was tough and didn't give violators any breaks.

The night he was murdered was just like every other night that he went out to find poachers. Poachers were usually doing one of two things: either setting traps out of season or trapping without a license. On October 20, at 9:00 a.m., Schmeltz and Hoff left for the Carp River just north of Negaunee to check on recent reports of illegal muskrat trapping. Hoff was physically disabled: he had an artificial left leg and a disfigured right foot. Although he was crippled, Schmeltz relied on Hoff to accompany him on remote patrols. Besides being a trusted companion on the isolated road searches, Schmeltz felt that Hoff could give him assistance if he ever needed it. Hoff was restricted in what he could do, but keeping his buddy company in his pursuit of violators provided him with a life purpose. He didn't know it at the time, but accompanying Schmeltz that day was significant for law enforcement.

It was a typical cold, bleak October day, when one would rather be snuggled up next to a warm fireplace than sitting in the woods looking for violators. However, Schmeltz had a job to do, and he did it with determination. He was on a stake and not too far from his car. Hoff waited patiently for Schmeltz in the car as he had done many times before. He became concerned by midafternoon when Schmeltz had not returned. This was not typical. As darkness edged out the receding daylight, Hoff became alarmed. He didn't have the car keys, but he knew he had to get help. Hoff tottered painfully down the Carp River Road to the main road to Negaunee. He then hitched a ride to town to report that Schmeltz was missing. Two other conservation officers drove Hoff back to the site, where, in a short time, they heard the explosions.

Kivela related to authorities what happened the night of the murder. He said that he was walking along a ridge by the Carp River when he encountered Schmeltz. Kivela said he was carrying a .22 rifle when Schmeltz asked him if he had a gun permit. He said that he could not produce a gun permit because he left it at home. As a result, he said Schmeltz was about to confiscate his gun. Kivela said he did not want to lose his gun, and that's when he struck Schmeltz and knocked him to the ground. Kivela turned the gun on Schmeltz and shot twice, both times striking him near the heart. He said that he completely lost his head when he killed Schmeltz. The killing took place about 11:00 a.m. After he murdered Schmeltz, he towed the body to a nearby swamp and covered it with brush. Kivela was now concerned that someone might find the body and that it would lead to his arrest.

To prevent being found out, Kivela quickly came up with a plan—he would dynamite the body, thus eliminating evidence. He went back to his farm, got in his car and went to Ishpeming, where he purchased one

Andrew Schmeltz's grave marker in Ishpeming's cemetery. Raymond Kivela killed conservation officer Schmeltz fearing that he would take his hunting traps for violating the law. *Author's collection.*

hundred sticks of dynamite. Then he returned home and finished his farm chores. Later in the evening, he played the customary checkers with his dad and then went to bed around 9:00 p.m. But his day was far from done. At midnight, he stealthily left the house and slipped into the night. He returned to the murder site, where he placed seventy sticks of dynamite on the body and ignited it. Kivela thought a large blast would drive the body down deeper into the swamp—he was mistaken. Instead, the blast spewed human flesh 250 feet in all directions. He was now in a worse predicament. Kivela went back to his farm only to return a short time later to see if he could clean up the mess with two more charges of dynamite.

Judge Frank Bell sentenced Kivela to life in prison on December 14, 1936. He served time in four Michigan prisons before he was placed in the Newberry State Hospital (which was an institution for people with psychiatric disorders). Prison officials said Kivela had a long history of mental illness. In 1981, when Kivela was seventy-four, Governor William G. Milliken commuted his sentence. He spent his last years in a nursing home in Upper Michigan.

17
THE LIEUTENANT WITH A LÜGER

Army lieutenant Coleman Peterson guns down Mike Chenoweth, a Big Bay tavern owner.

On a warm summer evening on July 31, 1952, Lieutenant Coleman Peterson looked solemnly at his wife and said, "I want you to swear on this rosary what you just told me was true." Without hesitation, Charlotte Peterson placed her hand on the sacred beads and swore that she was telling the truth.

Attractive, auburn-haired Charlotte had just told her husband that Mike Chenoweth, owner of the Lumberjack Tavern in Big Bay and former state trooper, had raped her. With his wife's testimony documented to his satisfaction, he retrieved his .9mm lüger and proceeded to the Lumberjack Tavern. The tavern was only a quarter mile from Peterson's trailer in Big Bay's Perkins Park. At midnight, Peterson reached the tavern and went to the bar where Chenoweth was working. Without wavering, he reached over the bar and pumped five bullets into the defenseless Chenoweth, who fell to the floor in a pool of blood; he died almost instantly.

Chenoweth was an excellent shot and kept guns at the bar, but the surprise attack didn't give him time to go for a gun. Peterson was probably unaware that Chenoweth was an expert marksman, but it is doubtful that would have made a difference. He committed the murder in the heat of anger, and nothing was going to stop him. Bartender Bud Wentzel stopped Peterson leaving the tavern. Peterson stared coldly at Wentzel and said, "Do you want one in the head?" Wentzel wisely let Peterson continue on.

Former state trooper Mike Chenoweth was gunned down in his bar, the Lumberjack Tavern, in 1952 by an angry husband. *Superior View Studio.*

The firing of the pistol sent bar patrons scurrying in all directions. Ken Goldsworthy, who just moments earlier had been sitting with Chenoweth, said, "All hell broke loose, and people were running everywhere. Several men ran into the women's bathroom."

Peterson returned to his trailer and told his wife that he just shot Chenoweth and that she should call Sheriff Marsh.

The events leading to the murder were provocative and sizzled the public's imagination. The tantalizing details wrapped the community in both horror and delight. Wanton sex, a jealous husband and a stunning lady were all the ingredients needed to stroke the shameless curiosity of the locals.

Earlier on that fateful evening, about 9:00 p.m., Charlotte Peterson bid her husband goodbye, left their trailer and walked to the Lumberjack to get a six-pack of beer. At the bar, Charlotte decided to have some drinks and play shuffleboard with Chenoweth. Peterson took off her shoes to gain leverage at the table—to the delight of the male patrons. Bud Wentzel said her behavior was considered "unlady-like." The early 1950s was not Victorian in moral values, but by later standards, Charlotte's behavior would not have been given a second thought.

After two and half hours in the bar, Peterson was ready to return home. According to her, Chenoweth offered her a ride, and at first she declined but later agreed to his offer. According to her, he did not take her home but instead pulled into a side road near the park and raped her. She said that she told Chenoweth that her husband would kill him if he found out.

Marquette resident Ken Goldsworthy revisited the Lumberjack
Tavern, where he witnessed the Chenoweth murder fifty years earlier.
Author's collection.

Chenoweth replied, "He doesn't have the guts. I'm not worried about
him—he's just a sissy." She said she left the car with a flashlight and, with
George, her shorthaired terrier, went back to the trailer.

Charlotte said she was screaming and crying when she entered the trailer.
This woke her sleeping husband. According to Coleman Peterson, he noted
the disheveled and bruised condition of his wife; her skirt was torn and her
panties were missing. He asked her what happened, and she told him. It took
a half hour for her to tell her husband. It was then that the incensed Peterson
took out the rosary.

The murder trial was held in September 1952 at the opulent, Beaux-Arts
Marquette County Courthouse. The elegant sandstone building constructed
in 1904 sits on a knoll overlooking Marquette's picturesque harbor. The

The opulent Marquette County courthouse where the Peterson murder trial took place; it later became the site for the filming of a movie based on the trial. *Author's collection.*

building's twenty-six-foot solid granite Doric columns at the entrance stand as able sentries, jealously guarding the building's portal. Inside, a white marble staircase gracefully sweeps up to the second floor. Impressive stained-glass windows and a detailed cornice frieze provide an elegant backdrop to the stair landing. At the end, massive dark-stained mahogany doors lead to the most imposing courtroom in Michigan's Upper Peninsula.

John Voelker, an Ishpeming attorney and former district attorney, was hired to defend Peterson. Voelker had served for fourteen years as district attorney but was defeated in a 1948 election. He felt empty and forlorn after this defeat and had the feeling the community had conspired to ridicule and humiliate him. In retrospect, the defeat was a blessing in disguise. Had he continued as a prosecuting attorney, he would have been on the opposite side in the Chenoweth murder, and his great blockbuster novel based on this case, *Anatomy of Murder*, might have never been written.

Voelker was facing Edmund Thomas, his nemesis, and the upstart attorney who beat him in the last election. Leaving nothing to chance in this high-profile murder trial, the prosecution solicited weighty Lansing assistant attorney general Irving Beattie to assist in the case. For Voelker, the trial was fraught with both vindication and fear. If he won the case against his adversary, glory would be his, but if he lost, there would be only humiliation.

Voelker had a difficult case. He had a defendant whose killing of a bar owner was witnessed by bar patrons. Voelker realized the only workable defense would be insanity. It was a long shot, but if it worked, the most his client would have to serve would be a period of time in a mental hospital.

Peterson played into the insanity defense with deftness. He said he remembered going to the bar with his gun and seeing Chenoweth at the bar but did not remember shooting him. The only way that he knew that he must have killed Chenoweth was when he got back to the trailer and discovered his gun was empty. To Voelker, Peterson's statements solidified the defense

Lieutenant Coleman Peterson, in defending his wife's honor, took his lüger and sought revenge. *Judith (Suvanto) Greene.*

of temporary insanity. The insanity plea might just work.

Voelker needed verification, though, that a rape did occur. However, that didn't happen. A medical evaluation did not show any evidence of a rape. Voelker was searching for anything that could make a jury sympathize with Peterson—a man who was simply defending his wife's honor. Charlotte's black and blue eyes were convincing, but were they inflicted during a rape or could her husband have done it in a fit a jealously? In addition, Peterson had a history of jealous rages when it came to his wife. If this were so, how could a defense attorney get around the crime not being premeditated? Voelker had an uphill battle.

On September 15, the trial began with the prosecution charging first-degree murder. It contended that forty to fifty minutes had elapsed between the time Peterson heard his wife's story and the time he shot Mike Chenoweth. This, the prosecution argued, gave Peterson time to plan the murder—a clear case of premeditation.

Charlotte Peterson went to the tavern where she shed her shoes and provocatively played pool to the delight of the male patrons. *Judith (Suvanto) Greene.*

In his opening statement, Voelker said, "The defense will show that the defendant was suddenly awakened, saw his wife in a dazed condition, sobbing, screaming, hysterical, her skirt ripped and her underpants missing; that his mind was in a turmoil…and that he decided to seek out Chenoweth and take him into custody…That he had legal right to go to the tavern, and…carry a loaded pistol; and that he was suffering from temporary insanity; that he was suffering from an irresistible impulse, and that he now has recovered." Voelker's phrase "irresistible impulse" would become legendary in legal circles.

Attorney John Voelker was hired to defend Coleman Peterson in what appeared to be an unwinnable case; however, the "country lawyer" was not to be out dueled. *Superior View Studio.*

Tempers flared in courtroom exchanges between Voelker and Beattie. In one instance, Voelker objected to Beattie's manner and line of questioning. Voelker let the jury know that Beattie was a hired gun—a big-city lawyer—and not one of their own. Beattie quickly shot back. "Just for the record, my home town is Marine City, Michigan, a smaller town than Marquette."

Ten days later, on September 25, after deliberating five hours, the jury of eleven men and one woman returned with a verdict of not guilty. Two Marquette physicians, Dr. Warren Lambert and Dr. Andrew Swinton, testified to Peterson's sanity and were satisfied that it was perfectly safe to have Peterson set free. Neither Lambert nor Swinton had psychiatric degrees.

John Voelker, the country lawyer with a homespun demeanor, had just won his greatest court victory.

To some, the verdict was a case of jury nullification—the prosecution had proven their case, but the jury chose to ignore the evidence and base its judgment on the position that Peterson was a man who was justified in defending his wife's honor.

The sensational 1952 murder trial quickly developed a life of its own. Voelker's novel *Anatomy of a Murder* was published in 1957 under the pen name of Robert Traver, and director Otto Preminger turned the bestseller into a hit movie in 1959. Filmed in Marquette and its environs, the city basked in the glory of being the temporary "tinsel town." Although the murder occurred over fifty years ago, it is something that Marquette and Big Bay residents still talk about at coffee clutches and cocktail parties.

18

BLOODSHED IN THE BALLROOM

Ballroom owner's body was riddled with bullets in midmorning shooting.

It was a nice summer morning in Marquette in July 1954. At 10:00 a.m., a car pulled up to the Brookton Ballroom and Minnie Club, a weekend dance joint located on the western periphery of the city. A man with a rifle got out of the car and proceeded to the front entrance door. A trio of carnival workers, lounging nearby under a shady tree, watched him walk up to the entrance.

He broke a pane of glass in the door, reached inside and unhooked the night latch. Inside, he went directly to the stairway that led upstairs to the second-floor apartment. The door was locked. The Brookton's owner, Jack Dalton, hearing sounds, approached the door. A blast from the rifle ripped through the door and hit Dalton in the gut. The intruder used an axe he grabbed from the first floor to smash down the second-floor door.

He stepped through the splintered door, followed a staggering Dalton into a bedroom occupied by Emil Fassbender—an employee of Dalton's—and pumped eight more bullets into Dalton's abdomen, head and legs. The assailant, his mission completed, left the carnage he created and returned to his home.

Jack Dalton was a large man weighing more than 250 pounds; he was no wimp. Longtime Marquette resident Bob York saw Dalton get into a fight with the bar regular. The man got Dalton down and started punching him. Dalton mocked his aggressor with a laugh, heaved him off and gave him a severe beating—you didn't fool around with Jack Dalton.

Dalton, left for dead, lived long enough to crawl to the phone, call the police and gasp, "I've been shot." He died by the time police arrived.

The three carnival workers who witnessed the man entering the Brookton at first were not alarmed. They thought the shots they heard were probably from a BB gun, which does not emit much sound. It did not take long, however, for the workers to realize that it was not a harmless BB gun they heard but the sounds of "shorts" from a .22 rifle. Fearing for their lives, they quickly fled—but not before noting the license plate number of the assailant's car.

Police identified the car as belonging to thirty-five-year-old Alfred Boucher. They proceeded to his home on Fisher Street.

Boucher was no stranger to the police. Neighbors had called the police on several occasions, reporting that he was outside carrying a gun. They were afraid that he was going to harm someone. However, by the time the police arrived to check out the complaint, Boucher was no longer brandishing a weapon.

This time, the police were more alarmed. A murder had occurred, and Boucher may have been the killer.

When they arrived at Boucher's, they found him and the alleged murder weapon, a .22-caliber automatic rifle, in his possession. He surrendered without resistance. Boucher had no remorse over the shooting and acknowledged that he had killed Dalton. The motive: he said that Dalton had given his wife some "doped" drinks seven or eight years ago when she worked for him as waitress at the Brookton.

Despite the earlier calls to police, neighbors thought kindly of Boucher. One girl who was fifteen at the time of the murder and lived only a few houses away said on most occasions he was pleasant to be around. She said, "He was really nice, and often he came down and took me and brother for a ride in his car. He knew our family didn't have a car, and we really like going with him."

Marquette resident Walt Cook said he and Boucher played on the same softball team in the late 1940s. Cook said, "Alfred was a quiet guy—kind of low-keyed—and a decent softball player; he never said too much."

Neither Boucher nor his wife, Mable, had been in the Brookton for some time. Boucher had been employed as a painter-decorator. He had five children ranging from several weeks to thirteen years.

Prosecuting Attorney Edmund J. Thomas charged Boucher with first-degree murder. Prior to the trial, however, the first-degree murder charge was tossed out when two doctors declared Boucher insane and unable to stand

The Brookton Ballroom was the hot spot for dancing to the Big Band sounds from the 1920s through the 1950s. *Superior View Studio.*

trial. Boucher was sent to the Ionia Michigan Asylum for Insane Criminals. (The name of the hospital was considered objectionable, as all the patients in the hospital were not criminals. As a result, the state legislature changed the name to the Ionia State Hospital. The hospital was used for the treatment of mentally ill prisoners. In 1972, the hospital became part of a larger prison complex and was renamed the Riverside Correctional Facility.)

Dalton was a native of Cheboygan, Michigan; he came to Marquette in 1945 and purchased the Brookton Ballroom and Minnie Club. The building was owned by Maude Sambrook and Clare Harrington. They combined the last syllable of each name (brook-ton) for the club name.

Prior to Dalton's arrival in Marquette, he was employed by the state as a tax administrator.

The Brookton Ballroom and Minnie Club quietly slipped into the pages of history and no longer exists. During its heyday, Marquette resident Kathryn Carlson said, "It was the hot spot; the place to be for dancing on Saturday night." Bob Moore, renowned Marquette trumpet virtuoso, played at the Brookton Ballroom with bands that thrived on the smooth sounds of the Big Bands—tunes that effortlessly floated to the dancers spinning around the floor, unconscious to everything but the rich sounds of the melody.

Visitors to the ballroom and Minnie Club would often find Dalton sitting in the same place at the end of the bar. One patron said he was friendly and easily engaged in conversation. Dalton was noted to have various hand gestures that he used to alert the staff to what he wanted.

The ballroom was upstairs in the two-story structure, and that was the location of the dance floor. Around the dance floor was an elevated platform; below the platform was the dance area that had the dubious title of the "snake pit." Those under the legal drinking age were permitted in the ballroom but not downstairs in the Minnie Club, where there was a bar. If a minor was lucky, he or she may have been able to sneak a beer in the bar, if Dalton was not around. He meticulously carded anyone he suspected was under age.

Dalton, age fifty, was unmarried. His survivors included both parents and two sisters. Contentious legal battles ensued over Dalton's will. It pitted family member against family member. One will written in 1949 declared his sister, Elizabeth Rezatto, as the primary beneficiary. A second will written more than five years later in September 1954 declared Dalton's mother, Ann Dalton, as the primary beneficiary. The court eventually accepted the second will and declared Ann Dalton as the primary beneficiary.

After the dance hall and bar closed, the building housed several businesses. At one time, it served as a retail furniture outlet and later as a storage facility for a local appliance and furniture dealer. The aging dance hall, the mecca for light-footed hoofers, suffered a regrettable end and was torn down in 1995.

Thirteen years after the murder, in July 1967, Boucher was declared sane by the hospital and released. Prosecuting attorney Edward Quinnell did not pursue the case and noted, "It would not serve any purpose at this time."

After his return to Marquette, Boucher reunited with his wife and spent the remainder of his life in the city. He lived quietly in relative obscurity until his death in 1994 at the age of seventy-four.

19
DEATH ON A WILDERNESS ROAD

In 1956, Patricia Burdick, an attractive second grade teacher in Grand Marais, was murdered by Marquette Branch Prison parolee Leonard Lundberg.

Highway M-28 in Michigan's Upper Peninsula is a long, barren corridor of blacktop that winds its way across the north side of the isolated region. A particularly desolate and uninhabited stretch on this highway is from Seney to Munising. In that expanse, there is one paved highway off M-28 in Seney that heads north to Lake Superior's rugged shore. It is highway M-77, a twenty-six-mile wilderness road that is columned by a lush forest of mixed hardwoods and evergreens.

At the terminal end of M-77, or the road to earth's end, is Grand Marais, a quaint hamlet that at one time was a burgeoning fishing and lumber village. The out-of-the-way village hugs the shoreline where a breakwater protects the town from Lake Superior's brutal, ripping winds that ravage the village on bitter-cold December days.

Summers, however, are idyllic. There aren't any theaters, box stores or gambling casinos to distract one from inhaling the summer stillness that satisfies tourists seeking solitude. Life pivots around outdoor activities.

In the summer and fall, fishing and hunting are the recreational pursuits, but in the winter, high school basketball games become the community's focal point. Fishing is still important in the lazy summer months, but now it is mostly left to tourists and local die-hards who seek fresh lake trout and whitefish. Grand Marais has the quiet rhythm of a community going about

Patricia Burdick, an attractive twenty-one-year-old Grand Marais teacher, was murdered near Seney after visiting her mother in Sault Ste. Marie. *Judith (Suvanto) Greene.*

its business, impervious to the outside world. The extraordinary residents brave the stark winters and hard economic times, conditions that normally drive people to sunny retreats but here create a bond.

The Grand Marais School has ninety students and seven teachers. The residents are proud of their diminutive but high-quality school, which also serves as the focal point for community activities. For years, Friday night football games and neighborhood fish fries were about the most excitement one would find in the village. And that was just fine with the 350 year-round residents.

But all that changed on April 26, 1956, when a teacher was found bludgeoned to death. The murder of attractive twenty-one-year-old Patricia Burdick shocked the town's peaceful citizens and put them on notice that their secluded world was no longer safe from the violence of urbanized America.

Burdick had been a first-year grade school teacher for eight months. She was described as reserved and did little to draw attention. Her unassuming demeanor, though, did not shield her from predator and prison parolee thirty-five-year-old Leonard Lundberg.

On Sunday, April 22, Burdick returned from her weekend trek to her mother's (Eva Burdick) in Sault Ste. Marie, a town one hundred miles east of Grand Marais. Unlike most working women her age, she did not have a car and depended on others to provide transportation for her weekend jaunts. On that Sunday, William Dolozel, a Marquette resident who was transporting four girls from the Sault to Northern Michigan University in Marquette, offered Burdick a ride to Seney. She took the ride and was dropped off at the M-77 and M-28 intersection in Seney, after which Dolozel continued on to Marquette with his other passengers.

A short time later, George Niemi and his wife stopped to pick up the hitchhiking Burdick, who was wearing a red jacket and khaki slacks. The

The Seney site on M-77 where Burdick was hitchhiking north to Grand Marais when she was picked up by prison parolee Leonard Lundberg. *Author's collection.*

123

Niemis were only going part of the way to Grand Marais; as a result, Burdick declined their ride offer, perhaps fearing that she would be stranded in a place with little traffic.

Marquette Branch Prison parolee Leonard Lundberg was visiting relatives in Seney the Sunday night that Burdick was there. Sometime after 8:30 p.m., he spotted the stranded Burdick hitchhiking and picked her up. En route to Grand Marais, he pulled into a side road in a remote area with the intention of having sex with the young woman, but she resisted. Lundberg then had a burst of anger, retrieved a tire wrench from the car trunk and smashed in Burdick's skull. Then he left her clothed body under a pine tree with some brush and straw thrown over the corpse.

Lundberg then headed to Marquette and, along the way, deposited his bloody clothes in a ravine under a bridge near Munising. This was a critical mistake. In the pocket of his bloody clothes, a laundry ticket with his name on it would be discovered.

The next day, when Burdick didn't show up at work, school personnel immediately called her mother. Mrs. Burdick, suspecting something was wrong, immediately contacted the police.

For the next two days, sheriff's deputies, state police and conservation officers combed the woods in search of Burdick. Joining the search party of over one hundred were lumbermen, villagers and servicemen from nearby Kinchloe Air Force Base. A helicopter and two airplanes from the civil air patrol augmented the ground search party. But the massive search was fruitless.

On the third day, Lundberg's bloody clothing was found. This was the first solid lead that investigators had, and it was a good one. A subsequent check on Lundberg found that he was a parolee from Marquette Branch Prison, and he had been in Seney the previous weekend. A further assessment found that he did not report to work at Munising Wood Products that Monday. Red flags were popping up everywhere. With substantial evidence now in hand, the police went to Lundberg's home in Marquette to question him about Burdick. He denied that he knew anything about her. A subsequent examination of his car, however, revealed fresh bloodstains. This, along with verification that he was in Seney the night of Burdick's disappearance, was enough to arrest him.

At first, Lundberg told the police that the blood was from a deer that he struck with his car and that he tried to put the deer carcass in the front seat. The police didn't buy his almost laughable explanation. They continued to confront him, and soon he confessed to the murder of Patricia Burdick.

The following day, Lundberg directed the police to the isolated spot where he left her body. He agreed to take the police to the scene of the murder as long as he didn't have to get out of the car and look at her.

While lodged in the Schoolcraft County Jail and awaiting arraignment and trial, Lundberg attempted suicide. He slashed his arm with a piece of glass that he had hidden. The slash opened two large veins in his upper arm, causing profuse bleeding and then shock. He needed immediate medical attention and was transported to the Schoolcraft County Hospital, where he received two plasma transfusions and a pint of blood.

Lundberg said of his failed suicide attempt, "I guess I didn't succeed."

Schoolcraft prosecutor William J. Sheahan said Lundberg's attempted suicide was phony and that he was only trying to establish an insanity defense. However, Lundberg had anticipated success in taking his life and left three letters. In one to a relative he wrote, "There was no reason for killing that girl, but sorrow won't bring her back."

Lundberg opted for a bench trial at the Schoolcraft County Courthouse. This meant there would not be a jury and that Judge Nebel would decide Lundberg's guilt or innocence, as well as the length of his sentence if he was determined guilty. It was a swift trial lasting only two days. The charge was first-degree murder, but Lundberg protested the charge and said it should be second degree. First degree necessitates premeditation, and Lundberg said the murder was not premeditated but an "explosion of anger." Lundberg's assessment was legally sound; however, the prosecution and citizens were in no mood to entertain anything that might give Lundberg anything less than a life sentence. His court-appointed attorney G.S. Johnson apparently did not contest the charge.

One of the key witnesses for the prosecution was forensic expert Dr. Clarence E. Muehberger, who testified that the red hair fibers similar to those in the coat worn by Burdick when she was killed were found on a pair of Lundberg's blue trousers.

A guilty decision was a foregone conclusion. In administering the sentence, Judge Nebel said, "You are a waster both with yourself and the people around you. " When Nebel asked if he had anything to say, Lundberg responded, "The slaying was not premeditated, but done in a burst of anger." It didn't matter what he said; he was going to prison for life. Eva Burdick wept quietly in the courtroom as the guilty verdict was read.

Lundberg was sent to Marquette Branch Prison to serve out his time. Guards who supervised Lundberg while he was in prison said he was a model prisoner and never gave them any trouble.

What became most remarkable is what Lundberg did while in prison. From being a burglar and murderer, he became an astute legal scholar. In spite of the fact that he had only an eighth grade education, he immersed himself in law and became a respected and serious legal advocate for other inmates. Other prisoners sought him out to prepare legal documentation for appeals or whatever legal advice they needed. Attorneys marveled at his competency, and many said that his lawyering skills were superior to some lawyers who were practicing law on the outside. If anyone reinvented himself for the better it was Leonard Lundberg.

In addition to working as a clerk in the prison store, Lundberg found time to become an ordained chaplain. When he was not busy clerking, lawyering or serving the spiritual needs of other inmates he made quality jewelry that he sold in the prison gift shop.

After serving twenty-one years in Marquette's prison, Lundberg was released in 1977 and moved to New York with his wife, whom he married while in prison. *Patricia Lundberg.*

His jewelry sideline led to outside contacts, one of whom was Patricia Montresor, a woman from upstate New York who had polio and who was also a jeweler. She began corresponding with Lundberg while he was in prison. This eventually blossomed into a romance that led to a marriage, which took place in the Marquette Branch Prison chapel in 1973. While in Marquette, the new Mrs. Lundberg stayed in the convent of the Sisters of Saint Paul De Chartres. She remarked to resident nun Sister Mary Ann Laurin, "I'm probably the only woman alive who spent her wedding night in a convent."

With a diligent effort by his wife and his attorney,

Lundberg, after serving twenty-one years in prison, was released in 1977. Mrs. Lundberg attributed prayer as the single most important thing that made the parole happen. The couple left Marquette and moved to Brooklyn, New York. Later, they moved to upstate New York. She saw her husband as a bright and caring man who after release from prison gave much time to charitable causes.

In 1999, Leonard Lundberg died in New York at the age of seventy-nine.

20
THE UNSOLVED SLASHING

The mutilated body of Paul Girard was found on a grave site with a slit throat and over forty gash wounds.

The mutilated body of Paul Girard, thirty-four, was found lying face up, not far from Charlie Kawbawgam's grave at the east side of the Presque Isle Park in Marquette. Over forty gashes mutilated his body, and his throat had been slit. The pattern and number of wounds suggested that the killer was frenzied, stabbing over and over again. Evidence indicated that a struggle had taken place fifteen to thirty feet from the body.

Girard had been murdered sometime after 3:30 a.m. on September 30, 1988.

An elderly woman had seen the body earlier but failed to report it, saying she thought it was a mannequin, part of a college prank. Another passerby reported it to the police at 10:15 a.m.

Little physical evidence was found at the scene. A jackknife near the body was determined to be Girard's, but it was not the murder weapon and didn't provide any clues. Girard's car was nearby in the Presque Isle marina parking lot. His car keys and wallet were never found. There was considerable blood, but it was all Girard's. The lack of evidence and no witnesses made the murder a nightmare to solve.

Then, the police received a break. Someone reported seeing a man between twenty and twenty-four years old wearing a dark jacket and tan pants walking down Lakeshore Boulevard at 4:00 a.m. the night of the crime. The same man—later identified as being five feet, ten inches tall with dark hair and a moustache—had been seen a second time that night farther down the same street. Police quickly identified the suspect.

Interrogated at length, the suspect (whose name was never released) provided information the police felt that only someone at the scene could possibly know. His home and workplace were meticulously searched for evidence. But nothing was found.

The Michigan State Police forensic laboratory evaluated hair fiber and blood samples taken from the murder site. Enlisting all possible resources, the Marquette police consulted with a University of Michigan forensic pathologist to review the skimpy evidence. All available department personnel were marshaled in what became the most extensive investigation in the Marquette Police Department's

Paul Girard died in the prime of his life (thirty-four) in 1988. He was murdered on a cold autumn night in Marquette's Presque Isle Park. *Mary Stiles.*

history. Most nonviolent police cases (bad checks, theft, etc.) were assigned to a single detective so the remaining detectives and officers could concentrate on the Girard case. More than a dozen detectives spent long hours trying to solve the murder. Marquette police detective Sal Sarvello said the police followed up on over two hundred tips but with little success. The case was difficult to solve because of the lack of evidence. Sarvello said, "It occurred in the middle of the night, so there's less physical evidence."

Sarvello believed that whoever committed the crime might have altered his behavior. Drastic changes in behavior are not uncommon for someone who just committed a crime. Sarvello said that perhaps his drinking increased or that he quit his job.

To stimulate community responses for information, a $2,000 reward was offered that authorities hoped would lead to an arrest. The reward was never collected.

The police theorized the murder was linked to Girard's lifestyle. Detective Mike Angeli, who was on the city police force about a year when the murder occurred, said, "Because of Girard's gay lifestyle he was well known to the police. He was often victimized by those that opposed the way he lived." Neighbors near his home on South Division Street reported guests coming and going at all hours. They also heard epithets shouted at his home from passing cars. Authorities felt the murder was a result of "gay bashing." In 1984, there were four confirmed gay murders in the state of Michigan. Some crime experts felt someone who had repressed homosexual desires might have committed the murder.

Girard grew up on a close-knit family farm near Carlsend, a small settlement twenty miles south of Marquette. His parents, Ernest and Adeline, raised beef cattle and had vegetable gardens in the idyllic setting. Although farming was not the primary source of income, it did provide the family with meat and vegetables. Girard's sisters, Sue (Girard-Jackson) and Mary (Stiles), described their upbringing as typical in rural Upper Michigan. Mary said, "We were just a normal family and didn't see ourselves any different from other families." While growing up, Paul often helped his father at a sawmill that was on the property. Sue and Mary said Paul was industrious and that his father was pleased when Paul labored with him at the mill.

The sisters had a close attachment to their brother. Sue said, "Paul was a great brother, and he would give anyone the shirt off his back." As a child, he loved to play with cars and enjoyed tinkering with anything mechanical. This interest served him well in adulthood. At B&D, a rental and sales shop in South Marquette, he repaired small engines. It was the ideal setting for using his mechanical skills. Girard could take an old and broken lawn mower and have it purring in no time.

Sue and Mary said Paul was a joy to be around, and this was particularly true when they shared Sunday dinner. Mary remarked, "He was witty and with an infectious laugh; he was fun to be around." The sisters had a deep affection for their brother and view what happened to him over twenty years ago a travesty for which there is no closure.

Months passed and then years, and the trail got colder. No new evidence was uncovered and police activity diminished, but the case remained an active, unsolved murder.

Speculation is that the murderer's identity is known, but police lack evidence to bring the case to the county prosecutor. The suspect, police say, has since moved out of the area.

Below the surface of the murder site, Ojibwa chief Charlie Kawbawgam rests in stoic silence. Two decades later, after that cold autumn night, the cutthroat is still at large, enjoying what life has to offer. Maybe periodically he glances uneasily over his shoulder, unsure of when the police may come knocking.

An unsolved murder always irks and frustrates law enforcement, but unsolved murders are common. Forty-eight percent of all murders in the United States are not solved. In a recent year in San Francisco, only 26 percent of the city's murders were solved. The Marquette police are unhappy that they did not bring Girard's murderer to justice, but they are not alone in failing to find a killer with only minimal evidence.

What left the Marquette police most exasperated was that they

Top: Paul Girard's body was found not far from Charlie Kawbawgam's grave in Presque Isle Park in Marquette. The murderer was never found. *Author's collection.*

Right: Mike Angeli, Marquette's chief of police, said, "The Girard murder is still an open case, and we will continue to follow any new leads." *Author's collection.*

almost had the killer in their grasp, but lack of evidence prevented an arrest and trial. Twenty-five years later, it still sticks in the department's craw.

The sensational headlines that dominated the papers told only part of the Paul Girard story. He was more than what the headlines blared; he was a decent human being who worked hard and had a loving family and caring friends.

Sal Sarvello, who was a detective on the case, said, "I believe there are at least one or two people in this area that still have knowledge of the murder. It hasn't been put away and forgotten."

Assistant prosecutor Peter Plummer, who worked the case, said, "Sometimes it takes years to develop evidence. Hurrying these cases does more harm than good." Perhaps there still is a chance that the "night slasher" will be caught.

21

PORTAGE CANAL CARNAGE

David Allen Goodreau, a churchgoing man of God, had a secret—a dark secret.

Houghton–(June 26, 1991) A decomposing female body was found by a fisherman in the Portage Canal yesterday. The canal is a waterway that cuts through the Keweenaw Peninsula, with both entry and exit on Lake Superior. Her decaying body had been floating in the waterway for fifteen days. The U.S. Coast Guard recovered her body from the canal after receiving a tip from a fisherman. She was identified as Kathy Nankervis, twenty, a L'Anse resident and the mother of two young children. She had cerebral palsy and was moderately disabled.

Houghton–(January 21, 1992) On a frosty winter night in Houghton, the body of Michigan Technological University (MTU) coed Jodi Watts, nineteen, was discovered in the early hours of the morning. Watts had been raped and stabbed in a parking ramp near the Subway restaurant in downtown Houghton. Watts, bloody and near death, managed to crawl in the snow 150 feet to a nearby street where a passerby on a bike discovered her. The biker covered her partially clad body and then reported the incident to police. When the police arrived, Watts was still alive, but she died shortly after being transported to the Portage View Hospital.

He never drank or smoked. He raised two delightful children and faithfully attended church. He had a job that helped others, and he had amiable chats with the neighbors. But David Allen Goodreau had everybody fooled—he was a killer; he would kill and then kill again. Kathy Nankervis

Attractive Jodi Watts, a former high school track star and nighttime jogger, was raped and murdered in Houghton on a cold winter evening. *Judith (Suwanto) Greene.*

and Jodi Watts were victims of the mild-mannered and unassuming David Allen Goodreau, a state social worker and caring father from Hancock.

He hardly looked or acted like a serial rapist and killer. A spiritual man, Goodreau and his wife attended the Calvary Baptist Church and played softball in the church league. He had been employed by the state since 1978, and he was one of two field workers in the Houghton County area.

In 1973, Goodreau graduated from Houghton High School, where he was an honors student and excelled in basketball and golf. He then attended Michigan Technological University (MTU), where he obtained a baccalaureate degree in forestry. Shortly after graduation, he married and left the area. He held jobs in Aurora, Illinois, and in downstate Michigan before returning to the Upper Peninsula. But Goodreau had a dark side that he hid for years. He buried his demonic nature, but eventually, his sinister side emerged.

Kathy Nankervis stood at five feet, two inches tall and weighed 115 pounds. She was a Social Security recipient, the mother of two children and a client of Goodreau's. He abducted Nankervis from her home on June 12, 1991, after peeking through her window and seeing her sleeping naked on a couch. He entered her house and bound her with duct tape and then took to her to the Lily Pond area of the Portage Canal. Goodreau said that he drowned her in the Lilly Pond, but her body resurfaced. He took her out of the water and repeatedly stabbed her, assuming that a release of air in her body would allow her to sink. He did not, however, puncture her stomach,

The Lily Pond area of the portage canal where the body of Kathryn Nankervis was found by a fisherman on June 26, 1991. *Author's collection.*

and the gasses that it contained later raised her to the surface. Two weeks later, a fisherman discovered her floating body in the canal.

When Nankervis was first reported missing by her family, authorities were not sure if they had a missing person case, a homicide or a suicide. Friends reported that Nankervis was recently depressed about having two children

The downtown parking ramp in Houghton where the body of Jodi Watts was found in the early morning hours of January 21, 1992. *Author's collection.*

and little social life. She had cerebral palsy that resulted in slurred speech and an awkward gait. The discovery of her body, however, made it quite clear to the police what they had on their hands.

In January 1992, just seven months after the Nankervis murder, Goodreau struck again. Jodi Watts was an attractive and popular co-ed on MTU's campus. The former high school track star was studying biology at the university, where her father was an administrator.

While jogging in the late night hours on a cold winter evening, Goodreau grabbed Watts near the Houghton municipal parking garage, adjacent to the Subway shop on Shelden Avenue. He hauled her farther into the garage, where he raped and brutally stabbed her. Goodreau suspected that she recognized him, and he knew that he would have to kill her to avoid being caught.

Goodreau, if nothing else, had audacity; he murdered Watts within one hundred feet of the police station.

This was the second murder in the area in a seven-month period and sent shock waves through the community. Women in the area began locking their doors, something they hadn't always done before the Watts and Nankervis murders.

MTU took quick action in the wake of the Watts slaying. Reluctantly, the university president authorized campus police to carry firearms, feeling it was imperative in order to provide added security on campus. The community was now on high alert.

Grief and shock emanated from the Houghton area with the slaying of Jodi Watts. Pastor of the Good Shepherd Lutheran Church Chris Heavner said, "She was a good person. Bubbly, smiling, didn't let things get her down." Jodi's high school friend Shannon Hanson, after learning of the murder, said, "I just cried and cried and thought why her." Steve Markey, a vice-president of Caesar's Pizza in Houghton, said, "Jodi did an outstanding job for us, she was great with customers. This is such a terrible tragedy."

The local Kiwanis Club, in hopes that it would lead to the killer's arrest, offered a $10,000 reward.

Police chief Ralph Raffaelli of Houghton said that these murders were the first in over twenty-five years in the county.

With few clues, both murders went unsolved for a longer period than the local police would have liked. As a result, the FBI was enlisted to assist in solving the double homicide. Like others before, an FBI profiler felt that the two murders might be related, only because it was unlikely that you would have two murderers killing at the same time in a sparsely populated area. In addition, the profiler said the perpetrator was probably physically strong, hated women and was most likely a local resident.

Investigators chased down five hundred leads over a thirty-state area but still came up with nothing until June 24, 1993, when a Hancock woman reported a break-in at her apartment at 2:30 a.m. They didn't know it at the time, but that break-in would unravel the Nankervis and Watts murders.

The police quickly responded to the forced entry and found Houghton social worker David Goodreau near the site of the apartment. Goodreau was immediately arrested, and within a short of time, much to the investigators' surprise, he confessed to the murders. Goodreau's wife and children were at a Bible study camp at the time of the apartment break-in.

For his defense, Goodreau hired Marquette attorney Mark Wisti. With Goodreau already having confessed to the murder, Wisti was limited in his options of a defense strategy. An insanity defense appeared to be the most plausible choice. Insanity is difficult to prove under the best conditions. Few lawyers advocate using a mental illness argument because it is rarely successful and extensive psychiatric evaluations are necessary.

Goodreau's initial exam by the state did not help his position, and he was declared competent to stand trial. The defense then had a second psychiatric

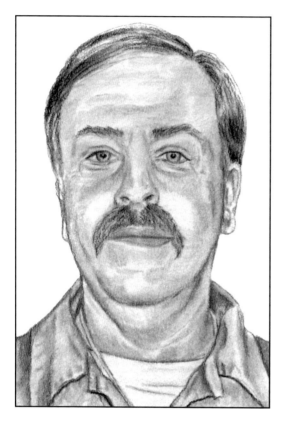

David Allen Goodreau, a Houghton County social worker and a religious man, murdered Jodi Watts and Kathryn Nankervis in the early 1990s. *Judith (Suvanto) Greene.*

examination conducted by a Marquette psychologist. This exam refuted the findings of the first psychological assessment. As a result, a third exam was conducted, and it affirmed his sanity.

Prosecutor Douglas Edwards said, "We had a beautiful confession, there was no chance of acquittal. The man claims to be religious, and he thought it [pleading guilty] was the right thing to do."

Goodreau pleaded guilty and had a bench trial in Houghton. A bench trial does not have a jury, and the judge makes a ruling of guilt or innocence and determines the sentence. During the trial, Goodreau serenely described the killing of Nankervis and Watts; in his discourse, he was relaxed and indifferent. At the end of the trial, Judge Garfield asked Goodreau if he had reflected on the charges. Goodreau responded, "I felt I was influenced by satanic forces at the time of the crimes."

James Lassila was a co-worker and a social worker who shared an office in Hancock with Goodreau. He lived about a mile from Goodreau, their children often played together and the men frequently carpooled to work. Lassila was incredulous when he heard about Goodreau's murders. He said, "We never saw this coming because he was so religious. When I was with him he was never anything but a gentleman. He never seemed like a violent person."

Goodreau's wife spoke with skepticism at the arrest of her husband. She said, "I knew he had been arrested, but that's not Dave." Goodreau excelled in keeping his hideous side well hidden—unbelievably, even from his wife.

Those who knew him said that he was an upstanding member of the community and no different from themselves. Mitch Lake, news director for WMPL-AM said, "He didn't come across as anything but a perfect upright citizen…friendly, soft-spoken." Goodreau at times was on the radio answering questions about Social Security on a local call-in talk show. Why Goodreau raped and murdered is not known. Most people view a murderer and rapist as just plain evil or, at best, a psychopathic lunatic.

> *They play one tune and dance to another.*
>
> —*John Clarke*

Was Goodreau responding to Darwinian logic and driven by a biological imperative to pass on his genes? Or was he committing these atrocious acts in a need to show his dominance over women? These speculations are open to debate, as his confession did not provide any definitive conclusion.

In the rural Upper Peninsula, rape occurs as it does in any metropolitan area, just with less frequency due to the sparse population. Data gathered by the Women's Safety Education Group has stated that one out of every four women on college campuses will be either raped or assaulted with the intent to rape. It states further that only 5 percent of all college rapes are reported and that only three out of every one hundred rapists are convicted. Tragically, Jodi Watts was one of these appalling statistics.

David Goodreau was sentenced to life in prison and is serving his time in the Straits Correctional Facility in Michigan. He has much time to pray now.

> *Everyone who does evil hates the light, and does not come to the light, lest his deeds should be exposed.*
>
> —*John 3:20*

22

SPOUSAL ASSASSIN

Bruce Moilanen attempted to disguise his wife's death as a hunting accident.

Ontonagon is a reposeful village located on the shores of Lake Superior in the northwest corner of Michigan's Upper Peninsula. In the winter the hamlet is subjected to driving blizzards when northwest winds howl off Lake Superior and drop several feet of snow. Only the courageous venture out on these stormy days, but they love it. On warm summer days, refreshing lake breezes sweep the shoreline and cool the lakeside village. It has the best of both worlds.

Not much happens in this peaceful town. Main Street has a sprinkling of watering holes visited by the locals, as well as a few mom-and-pop stores. And in the summer months, tourists visit the quaint village.

Bruce and Judy Moilanen were from Ontonagon but made their home in Marquette. They often visited their parents, who still resided in the village. This was particularly true on holidays.

On November 29, 1992, two days after Thanksgiving, the village solitude was shattered when an unheard-of event occurred—one of their own was murdered. Charismatic Judy Moilanen was found dead a short distance from her parents' home on Cherry Lane in rural Ontonagon. Her heart was ripped in half by a .30-06 rifle bullet. Finding Judy's body in the woods was unexpected but something that could be explained. It was hunting season, and an errant bullet that missed its target could have easily traveled beyond its quarry and inadvertently struck Moilanen. It was the time of year when blaze orange is fashionable and accidental shootings are not uncommon.

At 1:30 p.m. on a Sunday, Judy took her five dogs out for a walk. Later in the day and nearing dusk, Judy had not returned, and her mother, Mary Ann Blake, was starting to worry. In typical mother discomfort, Mary Ann took a brief walk in the surrounding woods in hopes of finding Judy but didn't have any luck. She returned to the house and asked Bill Dorvinan, a visiting neighbor, to search with her. It was getting dark, and it was not like Judy to be wandering in the woods at dusk. Her dogs were found, but Judy was nowhere to be seen.

They kept searching and spotted what appeared to be a body lying across a remote,

Bruce Moilanen on August 15, 1993, was convicted of murdering his wife. While jailed, Moilanen failed in an attempted escape. He was sentenced to life in prison. *Judith (Suvanto) Greene.*

sodden trail. Dorvinan and Blake cautiously approached the motionless form. They were horrified at their discovery; it was Judy Moilanen. Her feet were in a pool of water. Dorvinan turned her over and examined her blood-covered chest; she was dead. Mary Ann Blake shrieked in horror.

Judy Moilanen was born and raised in Ontonagon by religious parents. She had a normal upbringing in rural Upper Michigan. She loved the outdoors and was a skilled downhill skier who spent considerable time at nearby Porcupine Mountain Ski Hill, where she met her future husband, Bruce Moilanen.

They began a courtship that blossomed into marriage in June 1978. Judy's mother, Mary, was not enamored of her daughter marrying Bruce, but there was little she could do. Judy attended Northern Michigan University in Marquette and, after graduation, went to work at Marquette General

Hospital. She was employed as an assistant to the hospital administrator, and by all accounts, she was a valuable and well-liked employee.

Bruce Moilanen also grew up in Ontonagon and graduated from the local high school. His high school career was unremarkable, and the only evidence that he attended the school is a lone graduation picture. He attended Northern Michigan University and earned certification as an emergency medical technician. He was eventually employed by the EMS Department at Marquette General Hospital. His employment record was far from stellar. He was often late, and at times, he failed to show up. He was not well liked by other employees or by most who encountered him; he grated on nearly everyone. Whether he was aware of how unpleasant other people perceived him to be is uncertain. Shortly after Judy's death, he was fired by the hospital. He let others believe that he quit the hospital and that within a short period of time he would soon be wealthy.

Any death by firearms is investigated by the police. The Moilanen case was no exception. It appeared Judy's death was just one of those unfortunate hunting accidents, but a police investigation would have to substantiate that prior to certifying the cause of death.

State police crime investigator Bob Ball from the Calumet State Police post was the lead detective in the shooting and was ably assisted by Lieutenant Richard Goad and Sergeant Don Poupore of the Marquette post. In spite of these state police posts being in the remote Upper Peninsula, where few murders occur, these officers were highly skilled and determined.

Examining the crime scene at first yielded little information. There wasn't any forensic evidence—no gun, no bullets, no fingerprints and no DNA. What Ontonagon sheriff Tom Corda observed, however, was a bullet blaze on a tree not far from where the shooting occurred. But no bullet or shell casing was found near the tree. The police then sought the services of Dan Castle, an Ontonagon mine employee, who had a hobby of searching for hidden treasures with a metal detector. Castle repeatedly scanned the site but failed to find a bullet or a shell casing. Undaunted, Castle tried an unusual and creative method to find a bullet. He took a slingshot with marbles and fired them at the tree. Castle then observed where the marbles ricocheted. Over and over again, he searched the ground where the marbles had fallen and found nothing—finally his luck changed. Not far from the tree, he unearthed a foliage-covered .30-06 caliber bullet. At last, the police had something to work with.

In cases of a spouse death, the partner is always investigated. When a woman is murdered, 57 percent of the time either a husband or someone who knew her intimately is responsible. Red flags surfaced early in the Moilanen investigation.

One of the first things to ascertain was the time of death. Forensic evidence placed the time of death about 3:00 p.m., with a moderate open window at both ends. Bruce Moilanen easily established his whereabouts earlier in the day and also later that day, but he had difficulty verifying where he was at this time.

Investigators and others noted little remorse in Moilanen, and when there was sorrow, it looked contrived. A further investigation found that in the months prior to his wife's death, Moilanen had been making overtures to other women. Gayle Lampinen, a nurse at Portage Hospital, and Lee Ann Wsysocki, a Marquette resident and an employee at Marquette General Hospital, were the recipients of Moilanen's gratuitous attention. Wsysocki was a single parent raising a child and a good friend of Judy Moilanen. Neither Wsysocki nor Lampinen had any interest in Bruce Moilanen and considered him an annoyance. Regardless of the rebuffs he received from the women, he persistently contacted them.

The more the police investigated, the more it appeared that this was more than a hunting accident—and the evidence was clearly pointing at Bruce Moilanen. He knew the investigation was zeroing in on him, and he complained the police were harassing him. He continued to proclaim his innocence. Moilanen balked at taking a polygraph test. Arrangements were made several times for a lie-detector evaluation, but Moilanen never showed up or canceled just prior to the exam.

Finally, he took the test on April 23, with predictable results—he failed. Although not admissible in court, the results further convinced the detectives of Moilanen's guilt and increased the pressure on him. They continued to prod him when they told him they knew that he committed the murder. A broken man, Moilanen finally confessed to killing his wife. He was then jailed, and a trial date was set.

Prior to his trial, Moilanen attempted an escape from the Ontonagon County jail when he threw a powdery substance into a corrections officer's eyes and face. Moilanen then fled the jail to a nearby wooded area. Within a half hour, he was spotted on a dirt road and was pursued by the Ontonagon police. Moilanen did not give up without a fight. Gerald Kitzman, Ontonagon County sheriff, said, "He never really gave up. We had to tackle him and bring him down."

The Moilanen trial began in Marquette on November 19, 1993; it lasted until December 15. Prosecuting attorney Beth Paczesny, only twenty-six years of age, presented the case against Moilanen, while renowned attorney Tom Casselman was the defense attorney. Casselman's court presence is frequently abrasive and confrontational, while Paczesny's demeanor is low key. As a neophyte prosecutor trying her first big case, she must have felt somewhat intimidated by experienced and tenacious Casselman. But if she was, she didn't show it. Paczesny held her own and methodically presented her case.

Paczesny presented evidence that Bruce Moilanen had both motive and opportunity. She traced the acquisition of a .30-06 rifle to Moilanen's ownership, a weapon he acquired from a friend. She provided evidence as to his insolvency, and how he would receive over $300,000 in death benefits should his wife die an accidental death. Also, Paczesny pointed out that he was unable to account for his whereabouts at the time of his wife's death. The suspected love interest Moilanen had in Lampinen and Wsysocki was frosting on the case. Most damning, however, was Moilanen's confession to Bob Ball. The defense would have a difficult time explaining this. Casselman discredited the confession as one that was extracted from a tired and besieged defendant who would have confessed to anything to end the interrogation.

When the prosecution rested, it was Casselman's turn to present the defense case. He had subpoenaed twenty-nine witnesses, and the trial was expected to take another week. Casselman, however, surprised everyone, when he was asked by Judge Gotham to present his case. Casselman replied, "The defense rests." Even Judge Gotham was taken aback at this turn of

The Moilanen home in Beaver Grove near Marquette. Bruce Moilanen attempted to kill his wife in the home in what were "staged accidents." He failed in two attempts. *Author's collection.*

events. Up to this point, Casselman's case consisted largely of attacking prosecutor witnesses. This was how it would remain.

After six and a half hours, the jury reached a verdict. Court clerk Julienne Takala, in a quivering voice, read the verdict: "Bruce Robert Moilanen guilty of first-degree premeditated murder."

Moilanen showed no emotion at the verdict. He impassively stared ahead. When he killed his wife a year earlier, he sealed his fate. He would now spend the remainder of his life housed in Marquette Branch Prison with no possibility of parole. Ironically, his prison residence was just two miles from the home where he once lived in freedom.

23

DELUSIONAL DEFENDANT GETS LIFE SENTENCE

Nathan Hanna, a motor route driver for the Sault Evening News, *gunned down a colleague at work.*

> *They were saying, like I said, bondage and putting people in slavery and for sexual—people getting—okay, and then they loaded up and then they would get in debt to these people and then they would turn around and these people would take them over to a place across the sea where the main islands are over there. Then once they got them over there they had no rights as a citizen of the United States so they—turned them into bond slaves. Then they came back here. There are people back here that was already set up that if they got out of line or something they would work like the Mafia and they kill them if they didn't do what they did.*

That was the incoherent rambling of Nathan Hanna at his murder trial on July 23, 1998, in Sault Ste. Marie. Hanna's attorneys were pursuing an insanity defense for the man who had shot one of his colleagues while at work at the *Sault Evening News*. The prosecution, however, refuted the insanity plea and charged Hanna with first-degree murder.

> *The behavior of the insane is merely sane behavior, a bit exaggerated and distorted.*
>
> —*Aldous Huxley*

On a warm day in July, Hanna, a motor route driver for the *Evening News*, calmly approached *News* employee and circulation manager Anthony Gillespie in the newsroom. He then unleashed two shotgun blasts at Gillespie, killing him almost instantly. Richard Beadle, an advertising manager for the Sault paper, whose desk was near Gillespie's, witnessed the homicide. Beadle said he observed Hanna enter the room with a twelve-gauge shotgun and approach Gillespie's desk. Beadle said he didn't give it much thought as Hanna made small talk with him as he went by.

A gun brought to work would send shivers down the spine of most office workers, but this was the Upper Peninsula where hunting is the national sport. Someone proudly bringing a new shotgun to work to show co-workers would not be considered unusual. However, this was not the case with Hanna. Within a few moments, Beadle heard a shot and saw Gillespie fall to the floor. Beadle said Hanna then raised the gun and fired a second time, hitting Gillespie in the face. Another observer was receptionist Diane Glaz. Glaz said, "I first heard shots go off, and I looked up and saw body parts flying through the air; I was terrified." According to Beadle, Hanna then looked at him and another employee and walked out the front of the building slowly and deliberately.

After shooting Gillespie, Hanna left the newsroom and hid in the woods for three days. Following an exhaustive three-day search, Hanna was finally located on Baker Side Road, just off Three Mile Road. He did not surrender easily. When the police spotted a muttering Hanna walking down the rural road and carrying a gun, they commanded him to stop. Hanna, ignoring their commands, turned around and fired at the police. Three officers then returned fire, striking Hanna three times, in his chest, shoulder and leg. Hanna was seriously injured and was immediately taken to the War Memorial Hospital in the Sault, where he underwent seven hours of surgery.

During Hanna's confinement in the hospital, he confessed to the killing of Anthony Gillespie. Hanna's attorney, Elizabeth Church, attempted to have the hospital confession thrown out on the grounds of his physical and mental condition at the time. She also contended that he was deprived of council when she was not provided immediate access to him the day he confessed. In addition, she said he was not properly "Mirandized" (read his rights). The court rejected both defense motions and allowed the confession to be admitted at the trial. The court also said Hanna was properly read his rights. The confession would later provide Hanna legitimacy in requesting a retrial.

The prosecution charged Hanna with first-degree murder. Judge Lambros gave the jury instructions to an open murder charge. Under the open

The *Sault Evening News* building on Arlington Street in Sault Ste. Marie is the site of the murder of circulation manager Anthony Gillespie by Nathan Hanna, a contract motor carrier. *Author's collection.*

murder charge, the jury could consider six options: not guilty, first-degree murder, second-degree murder, guilty but mentally ill, not guilty but insane or manslaughter. Church agreed that her client had committed the murder and sought a conviction of not guilty but insane. She was convinced that he was delusional and met the insane criteria. Church said every mental health professional who came into contact with Hanna said he was not competent to stand trial. She said Hanna knew the killing was illegal, but not that it was morally wrong.

Using an insanity defense is dubious at best, and most lawyers know this. It is used in less than 1 percent of all murder cases, and only one-fourth of those are successful.

There are many problems associated with the insanity defense. First, definitions of insanity vary from state to state and the federal judiciary. Second, many of the statutes are confusing and difficult to understand. Furthermore, it is difficult for lay people to make a decision on insanity when attorneys, psychiatrists and judges cannot agree on exactly what constitutes insanity. Insanity as a legal term differs markedly from a psychiatric definition. One can be psychotic yet be legally sane. To add to the confusion, both the prosecution and defense solicit experts who support their opposing positions.

In the broadest legal terms, insanity is defined as not being able to tell right from wrong. In the Hanna case, it was determined by the court that he could tell right from wrong, even though at times his jumbled rambling speech was clearly delusional. Investigators interviewing Hanna felt that he knew he had done something wrong. Prosecutors contended that hiding in the woods for three days substantiated that he knew he did something wrong.

The murder trial began on July 25, 1999, and ended three days later. Hanna testified that he believed Gillespie to be the anti-Christ and that the deity had demanded him to kill Gillespie in order to save the world. The trial brimmed with psychiatric testimony, but little of it made an impact on the jury. The prosecution had a parade of witnesses, most testifying to the events of the day of the murder and the subsequent arrest. Much of this testimony was superfluous, as the defense did not question the mechanics of the murder; they were more concerned about Hanna's state of mind at the time of the slaying.

Gillespie's three children, who had contact with Hanna, said Hanna was not mentally disturbed. Church considered the children's testimony prejudicial.

The jury of nine men and three women deliberated for five hours and arrived at a verdict: Hanna was declared guilty but mentally ill. It was a compromise verdict between guilty and not guilty but insane. Observers felt that the jury wanted a conviction that would ensure Hanna would not be set free.

Hanna was sentenced to life without parole. He would be confined to a psychiatric prison with no possible release. Hanna's attorney sought and failed to get the insanity conviction and not the mentally ill conviction. If Hanna had received the insanity conviction he could have been released on a full recovery.

At the sentencing hearing, Judge Lambros said it was within the jury's right to reject the expert's opinions that Hanna was legally insane. The jury rejected psychiatric and psychological evaluations that concluded Hanna was not competent to stand trial.

At his sentencing hearing, Hanna said, "I'd like to say I'm sorry to the Gillespie family. I regret there is nothing that can be changed. That's all I have to say."

Hanna appealed his conviction to the Michigan State Court of Appeals. The appeals court affirmed the trial court's judgment that Hanna was guilty but mentally ill. The court rejected the defense's arguments that Hanna should have been convicted on an insanity charge. The court reasoned that: (1) Hanna knowingly waived his Miranda rights; (2) the lower court did not abuse its discretion in allowing Gillespie's three sons to testify as to Hanna's

Nathan Hanna, thirty-nine, was convicted of murdering Anthony Gillespie, forty-eight, in July 1998. He appealed and was granted a new trial. Again, he was found guilty. *Judith (Suvanto) Greene.*

sanity; and (3) the lower court's decision was sound.

Hanna's attorney then appealed to the Michigan Supreme Court. Again, the court reaffirmed the trial court's decision.

Hanna's attorney, still unhappy with the results, appealed to Judge Robert Bell's U.S. District Court. After a review of the case, Bell found the Hanna trial had a number of rulings that he considered in error. He ruled that Hanna's confession was not voluntary because he was medicated, in pain, suicidal and had not eaten for days. Bell also stated that former Chippewa County prosecutor Farrell Elliot had made prejudicial comments to the jury and that Hanna's defense attorney, Elizabeth Church, failed to object to those statements.

On November 6, 2007, after serving seven years in Michigan's Ionia State Prison, Hanna was returned to Judge Nicholas Lambros's Fiftieth Circuit Court for a hearing to schedule a new trial. Defense attorney Anthony Mark Dobias of Chippewa County said the trial would probably not take place until 2008. Dobias indicated that he needed time to allow for completion of medical evaluations for Hanna. Dobias replaced attorney Elizabeth Church, who was on leave. The federal court ruled that the trial must take place within ninety days of its ruling but agreed to give the defense an extension, as more time was needed for case preparation.

They sow the wind, and they shall reap the whirlwind.

—Hosea 8:7

In 2009, Hannah was again convicted of muder in a second trial and was sent back to prison. He died in prison in 2011 of pancreatic cancer; he was fifty-two.

24
A PICTURE-PERFECT PLAN FOR MURDER

Juanita Richardson plummets 140 feet to her death at Alger County's (Munising) Pictured Rocks.

Munising is a vacationer's delight. It's the crème de la crème of Lake Superior beauty. In the pleasant summer months, sightseers journey to the lakeside town to board ferryboats that cruise the nearby nationally famous Pictured Rocks Cliffs. The 140-foot sheer limestone cliffs jut skyward to their leafy crown. Their base of forbidding rock estuaries chiseled by relentless waves awes vacationers and is one of nature's wonders. Earth-tone hues on the precipitous cliffs embrace the early morning sun as Superior's icy waters carve intricate patterns on its isolated promontories. Peripheral hills wrap the lakeside town in a snugness that emanates security to its inhabitants. In the winter months, snowmobilers from the Midwest flock to the area where more than 250 inches of snow blanket the town.

Nothing much outside of this busy winter and summer tourist trade ever happens here. Murder—well that's something that you see on TV or in the movies or read about in the city papers that come on Sunday. Crime is minimal. A reckless youth might steal a car for a joy ride or a hapless soul get ticketed for drunk driving on Saturday night, but that's about as rowdy as it usually gets.

That all changed on June 22, 2006, when Juanita Richardson's broken body lay lifeless at the base of a Pictured Rocks lookout, where she had plummeted from a 140-foot cliff. It appeared to be a tragic accident and that Richardson

Juanita Richardson, forty-three, a secretary in the athletic department McBain High School, was on vacation in Michigan's Upper Peninsula when she met her untimely death. *Judith (Suvanto) Greene.*

had accidentally fallen to her death. It was the first suspected murder in Pictured Rocks history.

One of the Pictured Rocks tour boats was cruising the waters off Miners Castle just after Richardson's plunge. It was a blustery day with light rain and white caps battering the boat's bow. On board were Warren, Michigan resident Doris Crowl and her family. Crowl had loved visiting the Upper Peninsula ever since childhood and was delighted she could share her knowledge of the area with her husband and children. About 11:00 a.m., the ship's captain received a message that a woman had fallen from a cliff near Miners Castle. The captain maneuvered the ship as close to the rocky shoreline as he dared. Crowl said, "We could see this white jacket with all the red on it; this person wasn't moving." The size of the boat and the shallowness of the water prevented a rescue, but a police boat was en route from Munising. Unfortunately, Crowl told a reporter, "Seeing this woman's body at the base of the cliff will be a memory for the rest of their [her children's] lives; this is a sad remembrance of our vacation."

Juanita Richardson and her husband, Thomas, McBain, Michigan residents, were vacationing in the Upper Peninsula. Earlier, they had been in the Copper Country and were heading southeast when they stopped at Munising's Pictured Rocks to revisit what they called their "honeymoon spot." It was a small patch of land close to Miners Castle with a breathtaking view of Lake Superior.

Juanita was an active woman who took pride in her home and its surroundings. She loved gardening and landscaping, skills that suited her well in enhancing her family's new log home. Her children, Laceine, Lindsay and Levi, were a source of joy, as was her job at McBain High School as a secretary in the athletic department.

Thomas Richardson was born in Cadillac, Michigan, where he graduated from high school. He had several different jobs over the years from working at Four Winns, a boat company where he repaired boats, to his then current employment as a Federal Express driver in the Traverse City area.

Thomas Richardson, forty-six, was accused of pushing his wife, Juanita, off Munising's Pictured Rocks on June 22, 2006. *John Pepin.*

On the day of the cliff fall, Richardson told police and park staff that he left his wife near the lookout site and went to the visitor's center for a bathroom break. The visitor's center is about a half mile from the lookout. When he returned to the site, his wife was gone. Richardson said he crawled to the cliff's edge and peered over the side, only to see his wife's motionless body on the rocks below. He said he crawled to the edge because he was afraid of heights.

Later that day, Richardson told a different version of what happened. He now said when he returned from the visitor's center he saw her standing near the edge of the cliff and then she jumped, saying something like, "Oh my God," as she leaped to a certain death. Richardson said the reason that he did not initially tell authorities that she leaped to her death was because he was attempting to conceal her suicide from her children and her employer.

The following day, Richardson came up with a third rendition of Juanita's death. He told police that when he got back to the lookout, he saw his wife accidentally fall over the cliff's edge. Richardson was slowly becoming his own worst enemy.

Miners Castle at Pictured Rocks National Lakeshore juts into Lake Superior and is close to the site where Juanita Richardson plummeted to her death. *Author's collection.*

The Clevenger Visitor and Information Center at Miners Castle is where Thomas Richardson said he went for a bathroom break, leaving his wife near a cliff he called their "honeymoon spot." *Author's collection.*

Karen Bahrman, Alger County's "no nonsense" prosecuting attorney, successfully prosecuted Thomas Richardson for murder. It was her greatest court victory. *Author's collection.*

Richardson's contradictory stories on how his wife died raised the eyebrows of the police and indicated a further probe into Juanita's death was needed. Richardson at first freely talked with the police and was not aware that he was a suspect. However, within a short period of time, he knew that he was being targeted, but he returned home and optimistically thought his name would be cleared. As the investigation continued, more information came to light that convinced the police this was more than just an accident. After ten months of investigating, the police concluded that Thomas pushed Juanita off the cliff—it was murder.

On February 6, 2007, Thomas Richardson was arrested while at work and incarcerated in the Alger County jail in Munising.

Alger County prosecutor Karen Bahrman said, "There was a lot of risk in bringing this case to trial. You had a non-traditional defendant who had all the trappings of a normal life. This makes prosecution difficult, but I had no choice and had to do what was right."

On February 28, 2007, a preliminary hearing was held in Alger County's Ninety-third District Court in Munising to determine if the state had enough evidence to charge Richardson with murder. Bahrman litigated for the state, while Jason E. Elmore, a Cadillac lawyer, provided Richardson's defense. Judge Mark E. Luoma presided over the hearing.

Bahrman, fifty-one, was a seasoned prosecutor with twenty-five years of experience, the last six as Alger County's only prosecutor. Prior to Munising, she honed her skills in Marquette and Escanaba. The veteran barrister had a half dozen murder cases to her credit, the most recent was an inmate slaying at Shingleton's Camp Cusino. She was widely known as a no-nonsense prosecutor.

Early on, there was a question of who had jurisdiction over the case, the federal government, the state government or the county. It was determined that the state had jurisdiction because the federal lands in question were a unit of the National Park Service and not a national park.

The Alger County District Court building lacks the stately opulence that characterizes other county courts in the Upper Peninsula, but it does serve the needs of Alger County. The court was at capacity at the preliminary hearing, with more than forty people jammed into its church-like oak pews. Television cameras at the rear of the courtroom unobtrusively recorded the court proceedings.

Bahrman called twenty-three witnesses at the three-day preliminary hearing to support her contention that this was not a tragic accident, but murder. In addition to Richardson's inconsistent stories on how his wife died, Bahrman submitted collaborative evidence as to motive. The prosecutor's investigation revealed the Richardson marriage was rocky and that Juanita was considering divorce. Bahrman also noted that the couple was in serious debt and that Thomas Richardson was pursuing another love interest.

There wasn't any direct evidence that linked Richardson to his wife's death, but Bahrman felt the circumstantial evidence was enough to warrant a charge of open murder.

Elmore said Richardson did not push his wife off the cliff but instead that it was an unfortunate accident. The defense stated further that it was only natural that his recalling the event was inconsistent, as he was in emotional turmoil at the time and inconsistent statements would not be out of the ordinary. In addition, Elmore noted the lack of direct evidence linking Richardson to his wife's death. One of the few facts Elmore and Bahrman agreed on was that circumstantial evidence would be at the crux of the trial. Elmore's position, however, was significantly different than Bahrman's; he contended that the circumstantial evidence was not enough to charge his client with murder.

Bahrman, with her substantial height and dressed in a conservative black suit, exuded authority. With self-assuredness, she bantered with Elmore over a number of issues. Elmore looked boyish with his clipped hair and fair complexion. However, that belied his court presence; it was quickly evident that he was a capable attorney. His questions were sharp and direct, though at times he became mired in paperwork as he searched for information.

Richardson wore a dress shirt with a hint of yellow and a conservative brown tie. He stroked his neatly trimmed beard and took copious notes throughout the proceeding. He showed little emotion and occasionally bent over and engaged in brief conversations with his lawyer. Richardson wore dark glasses and said he needed them because his eyes were light sensitive due to a traumatic brain injury he suffered in 2002. Richardson's casual demeanor during the proceeding made it appear that he had not given serious thought to the possibility he could be spending the rest of his life in prison.

Judge Luoma in his black robe and thinning gray hair spoke softly yet confidently from the bench. The evidence threshold required at a preliminary hearing is minimal, and after three days of the hearing, Luoma concluded that the prosecution had presented enough evidence to bind Richardson over to circuit court to stand trial for murder. In hearing the decision, Richardson bent over in anguish and wept. He was bound over for trial and remained in jail. After the preliminary hearing, the case was moved to Alger County's Eleventh Judicial Circuit Court, where Judge Charles Stark presided.

Bahrman surprised the court several weeks after the preliminary examination—she demanded that defense attorney Elmore be removed from the case for intimidating a witness. Bahrman contended that Elmore threatened witness Kelli Brophy with prison and loss of child custody and that she could be considered an accessory to the murder. The prosecution contended that Brophy was Thomas Richardson's love interest and that her testimony could weaken the defense's case. Bahrman asserted that Elmore was attempting to negate her testimony through coercion. Elmore responded to the allegations by saying that he had a conversation with Brophy on July 31, 2006, but he emphatically stated, "There's no way I did anything to intimidate this woman." Judge Stark didn't see it Elmore's way and dismissed Elmore as the defense's attorney.

Elmore was not happy over his dismissal and sought redress through the appellate court. The case went to the appellate court and then to the

Attorney Karl Numinen examines some seven thousand pages of court testimony that the Richardson trial generated. *Author's collection.*

Michigan State Supreme Court. The higher court tossed the case back to the appellate court and directed it to render a decision. The appellate court reversed Stark's decision and reinstated Elmore. In Elmore's absence, Richardson hired attorney Karl Numinen of the Marquette law firm of Pence & Numinen. After Elmore's return, Richardson decided to retain both attorneys, with Numinen being the lead attorney and Elmore taking second chair. Articulate, impeccably dressed and well prepared, forty-four-year-old Numinen would be trying his first open murder case. He looked ready for the task.

Bahrman had additional concerns she brought to the court's attention. She wanted the court records to be sealed, stating that excessive publicity would be harmful to the case. Stark denied the request. Another point of contention that Bahrman had was Richardson's sunglasses. Bahrman said they were a distraction and that his eyes should be in full view so the jurors would better be able to determine the subtle nuances that eyes often reflect. Stark agreed, and Richardson was ordered to remove the sunglasses in court. She also asked the court's permission to bring the jurors to the site of the crime; she wanted them to see the cliff. Bahrman held that the site visitation was important and that just showing the photographs in the courtroom was not adequate. Stark rejected this request.

The combative attorney's duel continued when Numinen requested Stark remove Bahrman from the case. Numinen contended that Bahrman had illegally obtained records from Richardson's cell by using another inmate to steal them. Bahrman derided Numinen's allegations, saying it was "transparently retaliatory" after she successfully had Richardson's previous attorney removed from the case. She continued, "It is likely that Numinen's motion was for public consumption." Numinen was unsuccessful in getting Bahrman removed from the case, but he wasn't the only one trying to get rid of her.

In August 2007, Richardson was back in court for a pretrial evidentiary hearing. A cellmate of Richardson, Dylan Bonevelle, twenty-three, testified that Richardson had solicited him to kill Karen Bahrman. Richardson allegedly told Bonevelle, "He wished the pigs and hogs on Bahrman's farm would devour her and that he wouldn't cry a tear if she dropped dead." Bonevelle told Bahrman in the court, "He had a Corvette and a boat and was willing to trade for you." No charges were filed against Richardson for attempting to solicit a murder; prosecutors felt there was not enough evidence.

Numinen requested a change of venue because of the extensive coverage by the media. Stark agreed, and the trial was moved to Manistique, some thirty miles away. Numinen said, "I would have preferred the trial been moved a further distance from Munising, but Judge Stark kept it within his circuit district." At the same time, Stark removed himself as the trial judge, and it was reassigned to Probate Judge William Carmody. Numinen and Elmore sought Stark's removal, contending he was not up to the trial. Bahrman said she had no problem with Stark being the trial judge.

The trial began on March 3, 2008, twenty months after Juanita's death. With the pretrial issues finally settled, jury selection was next for the scheduled six-week trial. Numinen wanted jurors who had an education. He said, "They were more likely to examine the facts and less likely to make emotional judgments." Fifteen jurors were selected from the 114 who were called. Numinen dismissed 12, the maximum number allowed, and Bahrman dismissed 11. Two of the final 15 had college degrees. Three of the fifteen jurors were alternates and would be removed prior to deliberations. The court bailiff, drawing names out of a hat, would select those removed. Going into the trial, Numinen said, "I was very confident that we had a winnable case."

The prosecution had the first five weeks while the defense had the remaining week. Bahrman had 169 witnesses scheduled, while Numinen and Elmore had 93 for the defense. Not all would testify. The first week of the trial traced the sequence of events at the Pictured Rocks site. This included testimony from park rangers, park police and emergency medical personnel, who were first on the scene.

The heart of the trial, however, was Richardson's character. Bahrman attempted to establish that Richardson wanted his wife dead, while the defense argued that what happened was a tragic accident.

Through numerous witnesses, Bahrman explored the Richardsons' finances and revealed they had serious money problems. They built an opulent log home on waterfront property that was beyond their means and still owed $191,000 on it. In addition, the Richardsons had $27,000 of credit card and truck payment debt. Their total debt was $237,000. As a Federal Express driver, Richardson had a decent income, but it was not enough to sustain his lifestyle. This debt, Bahrman advocated, was one of the reasons Richardson wanted his wife dead. A $240,000 life insurance policy was just enough to bail him out.

Steve Vanderwall, a close friend of Thomas Richardson whose wife had recently died of cancer, testified to a conversation he had with him. Richardson knew when Vanderwall's wife died that he collected her life insurance and paid off his debts. He was envious of Vanderwall's financial windfall. Bahrman said Richardson believed the only way to get out of debt and pursue his new love interest was to kill his wife.

Bahrman continued with a number of witnesses who testified about the couple's rocky marriage. They separated in 1999 and reconciled in 2000. It was known by Juanita's friends that she was planning to divorce him as soon as their last child left the house. In June, their youngest, Levi, graduated from high school. If Juanita divorced Thomas, he would be left financially destitute.

Core to Bahrman's prosecution was Richardson's liaisons with Kelli Brophy, a woman he met while stopping in for coffee at the Quality Dairy, her place of employment. A number of witnesses testified that Richardson and Brophy had a relationship that was more than platonic. He was serious about the affair and reassured his new love that at some time he'd take care of her. Richardson and Brophy made 383 phone calls during the relationship, including one the night before Juanita's death. Purportedly, Richardson also told Brophy, "If anything ever happens he'd put a ring on her finger." Bahrman contended that Brophy was another reason that Richardson wanted his wife out of the way. Brophy, however, denied she and Richardson had a relationship and said they were only friends who talked about the Bible and scripture.

Marquette County medical examiner Randy Smith testified that Juanita Richardson died as a result of multiple injuries suffered during the fall. Smith could not establish whether she died as a result of an accident, suicide or murder. Juanita Richardson had a fractured neck and a bruised breastbone, Smith reported. "She had a lot of injuries on her neck that could have been caused by a variety of mechanisms," Smith said. His testimony was neither advantageous for the prosecution nor the defense but did establish what she died of, if not how it came about.

Bahrman, attempting to establish Thomas Richardson's culpability, called Douglas Kehl to testify on how he instructed Richardson in martial arts that included five chokeholds, of which one was a "carotid sleeper hold."

Juanita Richardson's father, Don Culver, also testified for the prosecution. Culver said after their separation he wanted his daughter to get out of the relationship and "not look back." Early in the Richardson marriage, he said his daughter had facial bruises she got from her husband. Culver said, "I'd kill him if it ever happened again."

After five weeks of prosecution testimony, Elmore and Numinen presented the defense's case. Prior to calling their first witness, Numinen argued for a dismissal of the charges, stating, "There is no evidence of causation." Judge

Carmody, however, denied an acquittal, saying that he "was not persuaded a jury could not find guilt beyond a reasonable doubt."

Attempting to discredit the prosecution's case, Numinen and Elmore had several of Richardson's friends and co-workers from Four Winns testify as to Richardson's character. Comments from supporters were positive. "He loved his family," "a man of high integrity," "easy to talk to" and "he didn't have anything to do with her death" were the range of comments solicited from the stand by those who believed in his innocence.

Not an uncommon defense strategy in a murder trial is to try to taint the character of the victim. This was the case in the Richardson trial as well when the defense called Molly Bassett to testify about two affairs that Juanita had during her marriage to Richardson. Bassett said Juanita told her about the affairs in confidence. She was reluctant to testify and did so only when Numinen subpoenaed her.

The defense submitted medical testimony on Juanita's use of the prescription drug Effexor that she once took for depression. A search of the house, requested by the defense in June 2007, resulted in finding a pill container of Effexor. The defense attempted to establish that Juanita was suffering from depression, thus making suicide seem more plausible. The prosecution countered that Juanita's use of Effexor was long ago and that she was no longer taking the drug. After her death, a toxicology report did not show any sign of drugs in her system.

The defense called psychologist Dr. Julianne Kirkham, an expert in neuropsychology who works at Marquette General Hospital, to testify on acute stress reaction. "Dilated pupil, rapid breathing, sweating, muscle cramps and nausea are symptoms of someone who is having an acute stress reaction," Kirkham said. She noted a park employee described Richardson as having some of these symptoms at the time of his wife's death. Kirkham said, "All of these symptoms suggest he was responding to something horrifying." She also stated that someone suffering from this disorder might be sensitive to light. Richardson wore sunglasses increasingly after his wife's death. Kirkham said she didn't think his symptoms were related to the traumatic brain injury that Richardson said he suffered years earlier.

Emotional and powerful testimony was elicited from Laceine Richardson, the eldest daughter. In a tearful testimony, Laceine described her childhood as carefree and parentally supportive. "They [her parents] would have done anything to make us happy," she said. Thomas Richardson teared up and put his head down during his daughter's dramatic testimony. Laceine said her father wasn't sleeping or eating much after her mother's death. She noted that she saw him crying one time when he was cutting the grass.

With the trial portion concluded, Carmody gave the jury instructions prior to their deliberations. He said they could consider four charges: first-degree murder, second-degree murder and voluntary or involuntary manslaughter. They must be unanimous in their decision; any split is a hung jury.

Public speculation on Richardson guilt or innocence ranged anywhere from "He's guilty as sin" to "No smoking gun—acquit." It was now up to the jury to decide whether Richardson would spend the rest of his life in prison. The jury began deliberations at 11:30 a.m. on Tuesday, April 15, 2008, and concluded at 5:30 p.m. that day with no decision. The jurors took a vote that afternoon with a seven-five split, seven saying guilty and five not guilty. They resumed deliberations on Wednesday morning, and at 3:10 p.m., after eleven hours of discussion, they reached a verdict. When the jury reassembled in the jury box, Carmody asked jury foreman Jeff Bolm to speak for the jurors. Bolm, a veneer mill employee, read from a sheet of paper: "We the jury find the defendant Thomas David Richardson guilty of murder in the first degree."

Thomas Richardson's children, stunned at the verdict, cried. Not only had they lost their mother, but they would now also lose their father.

Juanita Richardson's family wept and held one another.

Richardson was noticeably distressed as he exited the courtroom. He was taken to the Alger County jail to await sentencing on May 19, 2008.

Bahrman said, "I was more optimistic when the jury went into its second day, usually quick decisions are not good for the prosecution. The longer they take, the better."

The trial was exhaustive for both the prosecution and the defense. Numinen and Elmore stayed in Manistique for the duration of the trial. Numinen said, "We often left the courtroom at 6:00 p.m., went to our motel where we frequently worked until midnight, then slept for a few hours and were back in court by 6:00 a.m., getting ready for another day." Bahrman also stayed in Manistique for the trial.

Richardson was sentenced at Alger County Circuit Court, where a packed courtroom assembled for the last breath of the lengthy trial. Janette Ellens, Juanita's sister, spoke for her family. In measured comments and near tears, she held a large picture of Juanita and said, "God gave her to Mom and Dad to love, and they did." Ellens then looked at Richardson, "She worked hard but could never please you. I only hope that Juanita was oblivious to the evil in your heart."

Richardson spoke for the first time in court when Ellens finished her statements. Responding to her statements, Richardson said, "That was inaccurate but touching." He made additional comments on how much he loved Juanita and how good their marriage had become. He never admitted guilt.

There was little drama to Judge Carmody's expected sentencing, he followed the mandated state guidelines and remanded Richardson to life in prison without the possibility of parole.

Ellen, after the sentencing hearing, said, "I wanted to tell Thomas Richardson what I thought of him, but I was advised to keep it positive—it was Juanita's day. It was very difficult for me to do that with him sitting there."

Immediately after the sentencing, Richardson was interviewed by NBC's *Dateline*, where *Mining Journal* reporter John Pepin was present. He was then transported to Marquette Branch Prison, where he was processed and then sent to the Southeast Michigan prison in Jackson.

Elmore and Numinen said they would seek a new trial. Numinen said there were several areas that justified this. "The character issue was the thrust in the prosecution's case, and one cannot be convicted of a crime based solely on their character," he asserted.

There are no winners in murder. Juanita is dead, Thomas will spend the rest of his life in prison, Juanita's parents and sister are disconsolate over their loss and the children lost both their parents. Murder trials, unfortunately, create alignments of allegiance that disrupt both families and communities.

At the sentencing, Juanita's family wore purple shirts of solidarity with "Justice for Juanita" neatly embroidered over the heart of the shirt. Her children, however, sat on the defense side of the courtroom, with their father's parents, David and Meredith Richardson. The memories of Juanita may dim as the years go by, but those she touched will cherish remembrances, be it only for a lingering moment.

Munising has returned to its casual rhythm, where summer tour boats search out coastal beauty and winter snowmobiles hum in the winter paradise. The Richardson murder trial brought excitement to the city, not unlike what the Chenoweth (*Anatomy of Murder*) murder did to Marquette over fifty years ago. Chatter about the trial in the coffee shops diminishes as the years pass. And reporters and curious onlookers have vanished. The court drama is gone, but few residents will forget the happenings of what was a near picture-perfect murder.

BIBLIOGRAPHY

Angeli, Mike. Author interview, June 4, 2008.

Bahrman, Karen. Author interview, May 21, 1980.

Barfknecht, Gary W. *Murder, Michigan.* Davison, MI: Friede Publications, 1983.

Bohnak, Karl. *So Cold a Sky.* Negaunee, MI: Cold Sky Publications, 2006.

Brand, Scott. "Dobias to Represent Hanna in Murder Trial." *Sault Ste. Marie Evening News*, November 10, 2007.

————. "Nathan Hanna Guilty of Murder." *Sault Ste. Marie Evening News*, June 29, 1999.

Bright, Charles. *The Powers That Punish: Prison and Politics in the Era of the "Big House," 1920–1955.* Ann Arbor: University of Michigan Press, 1996.

Brock, Karen. *National Criminal Justice Service.* NCJ 183312. Washington, D.C.: Government Printing Office, 1999.

Bryce, George, LLD. "Sketch of the Life of John Tanner, A Famous Manitoba Scout, A Border Type." Manitoba Historical Society. *MHS Transactions* 1, no. 30 (1888).

Bibliography

Carlson, Kathryn. Author interview August 8, 2013.

Colombe, Lynn. "Confession Not End of Story." *Houghton Mining Gazette*, August 8, 1993.

Distel, Dave Lynn. *Hunt to Kill.* New York: Kensington Publishing Corp., 2005.

Daily Eagle-Star. "Chas Adams on Rack in the Erickson Trial." August 27, 1904.

————. "Erickson Arranged for Alleged Murder." August 26, 1904.

————. "Trial for Murder." February 4, 1905.

Daily Herald-Leader. "Erickson Case to be Bitterly Contested." January 21, 1905

————. "Penitentiary or Asylum for Girl Murder." January 18, 1928.

————. "Prosecution Rests Its Case, Detective Johnson Is Not Called." August 29, 1904.

————. "To Judge Erickson." February 6, 1905.

Escanaba Daily Press. "Defense Says Weina Killed John Malberg." January 15, 1919.

Escanaba Morning Press. "Anderson Held without Bail for Murder." November 17, 1918.

————. "Jury Will Get the Anderson Case before Night." November 15, 1918.

Esper, Mark. "Stagecoach Robbery Part of Range Folklore." *Ironwood Daily Globe*, August 25, 1988.

Evening Gazette. "Identify Bones in Murder Case Those of Human." October 24, 1919.

Flesher, John. "Houghton Still Struggles after Murder of Coed." *Ironwood Daily Globe*, January 16, 1993.

BIBLIOGRAPHY

Frank, Leonard Roy. *Quotationary.* New York: Random House, 2001.

Fuller, George N., ed. *Michigan History Magazine* 30: 268, 273.
Gladstone Delta Reporter. "Drunken Brawl at Kipling Ends in Death of One."
     November 12, 1918.

———. "Knife Believed to Have Killed Man Is Found." November 15, 1918.

———. "Witness Tells How Anderson Killed Victim." January 15, 1919.

Goldsworthy, Kenneth. Author interview, July 25, 2001.

Healy, Nick. "Husband's Murder Confession Will Be Allowed in Trial."
     Marquette Mining Journal, November 4, 1993.

———. "Moilanen Gets Life in Prison." *Marquette Mining Journal*, January
     22, 1994.

Herald Press. "Convict Leads State Police to Death Site." April 26, 1956.

Hoagland, Alice K. "The Boarding House Murders: Housing and American
     Ideals in Michigan's Copper Country 1913." *Journal of the Vernacular
     Architecture Forum* 2 (2004): 1–18.

Hornbogen, Daniel. Telephone interview, May 20, 2008.

Hoyum, Kim. "Murder at the Island." *Marquette Mining Journal*, September
     30, 2008.

Hunt, Mary Don. *Hunts' Guide to Michigan's Upper Peninsula*. Albion, MI:
     Midwestern Guides, 1997.

Ironwood Daily Globe. "Authorities Seek Missing Teacher." April 24, 1956.

———. "Chassell Man Confesses to Pair of Murders." July 2, 1992.

———. "Goodreau Pleads Guilty Wednesday." January 13, 1994.

———. "Innocent, Plea of Lundberg." June 18, 1956.

Bibliography

————. "No Leads in MTU Slaying." January 21, 1992.

————. "Paroled Convict Admits Killing Teacher." April 26, 1956.

————. "Suicide Attempt Fails for Accused Murderer." April 27, 1956.

————. "Teacher's Slayer Would Become an Outcast in Marquette Branch Prison." May 9, 1956.

————. "Verdict Expected in Lundberg Trial." June 20, 1956.

————. "Watts Reward Question Raised." July 8, 1993.

Johanson, Bruce H. *Murder and Mayhem*. Ontonagon, MI: Firesteel Publications, 1997.

Laurin, Sister Mary Ann. Telephone interview, October 23, 2007.

Lehto, Steve. *Death's Door*. Troy, MI: Momentum Books, 2006.

Lempesis, Andrew. Author interview, August 15, 2013.

Lempesis, Marilyn. Author interview, August 15, 2013.

Levra, Margaret. "Police Say Stranger May Have Slain Woman." *Ironwood Daily Globe*, April 20, 1956.

Longtine, Sonny. *Michigan's Upper Peninsula: Life, Legends, and Landmarks*. Marquette, MI: Sunnyside Publications, 2001.

Lowe, Kenneth. "Dynamite in the Swamp." *Michigan Out-of-Doors*, February 14, 1984.

————. "The Sands Plains Murders." *Michigan Out-Of-Doors*, February 12, 1984.

Marquette Mining Journal. "Account of Chenoweth Slaying Given in Circuit Court." September 16, 1952.

————. "Army Officer Held For Murder of Big Bay Tavern Proprietor." July 31, 1952.

————. "Cold War Between Voelker, Beattie." September 19, 1954.

————. "Dalton Proprietor of Brookton, Murdered." July 9, 1954.

————. "Dr. Hornbogen Is Instantly Killed; Men Trapped in Building." August 28, 1931.

————. "Four Are Stabbed in Marquette Branch Prison." December 12, 1921.

————. "Fourth Victim of Saturday Morning Shootings Passes." August 25, 1924.

————. "Governor, Other State Officials, Favor Death Law." December 13, 1921.

————. "Jackson Rules 2nd Dalton Will Valid." July 20, 1955.

————. "Last Chapter Written in Murder Case: Judge Frees Lt. Peterson From Custody." September 15, 1952.

————. "Law Officers Trek to Big Bay to Continue Investigation in Chenoweth Murder Case." July 31, 1952.

————. "Marquette Branch Prison Inmate Claims He Is Costliest in Michigan." May 19, 1975.

————. "No Foundation for Rumor of Prison Probe." August 28, 1931.

————. "Peterson Murder Trial Concluded." September 22, 1952.

————. "Sgt. Spratto Tells of His Investigation of Murder Case." September 17, 1952.

————. "Six Killed in Prison Riot." August 1931, 3–4.

————. "Slaying of Three Policemen in City in 1924 Recalled." August 22, 1964.

———. "Story of Alleged Assault, Rape Given by Mrs. Peterson." September 19, 1952.

———. "13 Year-Old Murder Case Dismissed." July 3, 1967.

Michigan Historical Commission. *Michigan\History Magazine* 30 (1946): 772.

Miller, Ann. Author interview, August 6, 2013.

Montresor, Patricia. Telephone interview, October 27, 2007.

Moore, Robert. Author interview, August 6, 2013.

News Palladium. "Slayer of Teacher Convicted." June 21, 1956.

New York Daily Tribune. "Murder of Mr. Schoolcraft." July 14, 1846.

Nicholson, Kenneth A. "Under Fire." The Dally-Jane Murders in Painesdale during the Copper Strike of 1913–1914. http://www.copperrange.org/strike.htm.

Numinen, Karl. Author interview, May 14, 1980.

Offender Tracking Information System (OTIS). Michigan Department of Corrections. http://www.michigan.gov/corrections/0,1607,7-119-1409---,00.html.

Pepin, John. "Motion Filed." *Marquette Mining Journal*, May 1, 2007.

———. "Prosecution Rests," *Marquette Mining Journal*, April 3, 2008.

———. "Psychologist Testifies in Richardson Case," *Marquette Mining Journal*, April 9, 2008.

———. "Richardson Accused of Targeting Prosecutor," *Marquette Mining Journal*, August 21, 2007, A1+ll.

Peterson, Greg. "Alleged Killer Back in Jail after Brief Escape." *Marquette Mining Journal*, August 1, 1993.

———. "Judge Denies Use of Experts in Murder Trial," *Marquette Mining Journal*, October 6, 2007.

Peterson, Paul. "Police Continue Watts Murder Investigation." *Houghton Mining Gazette*, January 27, 1992.

Pond v. People, 8 Mich. 150 (1860).

Reimann, Lewis C. *The Game Warden and the Poachers*. Ann Arbor, MI: Northwoods Publisher, 1959.

———. *Incredible Seney*. Ann Arbor, MI: Northwoods Publisher, 1953.

Riordan, John J. *The Dark Peninsula*. AuTrain, MI: Avery Color Studios, 1976.

Rydholm, Fred C. *Superior Heartland*. Marquette, MI: Rydholm Publishing, 1989.

Sargent, Bud. "The Book Remains Open on Unsolved Presque Isle Slaying." *Marquette Mining Journal*, September 30, 1992.

———. "Husband Charged in Ontonagon Shooting." *Marquette, Mining Journal*, April 25, 1993.

———. "Police Look to Experts," *Marquette Mining Journal*, October 23, 1988.

———. "Unsolved Slaying Nearly 1 Year Old." *Marquette Mining Journal*, September 24, 1988.

Sault Evening News. "Jim Harcourt's Story." July 27, 1891.

Sault Ste. Marie Evening News. "Daniel Dunn Is Dead." July 27, 1891.

———. "Hanna's Attorney to Seek Venue Change." August 18, 1998.

Starnes, Amy. "Goodreau Pleads Guilty." *Houghton Mining Gazette*, January 13, 1994.

State of Michigan: Court of Appeals. *People of the State of Michigan v. Nathan Paul Hanna.* November 27, 2001. No. 221555.

Steere, Joseph H. Sketch of Johan Tanner, Known as the "White Indian." *Michigan Pioneer and Historical Collections*, 22 (1899): 246–254.

Stevens, John. Author interview, June 6, 2013.

Storey, Jack. "Defense Opens Bid to Declare Hanna Insane." *Sault Ste. Marie Evening News*, June 25, 1999.

———. "Hanna Ruled Incompetent to Stand Trial for Murder." *Sault Ste. Marie Evening News*, September 4, 1998.

"Tales & Trails of Tro-La-Oz-Ken." A Bicentennial Publication of the Trout Lake Women's Club.

Thurner, Arthur W. *Rebels on the Range.* Lake Linden, MI: John J. Forster Press, 1984.

Veselenak, Aron J. *Michigan History Magazine* (May/June 1998).

Wikipedia. S.v. "Michigan Murders." http://en.wikipedia.org/wiki/Michigan_murders.

———. S.v. "Serial Killer." http://en.wikipedia.org/wiki/Serial_killer.

Wilson, Colin. *The History of Murder.* Edison, NJ: Castle Books, 2004.

Women's Safety Education Group. "National Safety Awareness Month." September 8, 2006.

York, Bill. Author interview, August 6, 2013.

ABOUT THE AUTHOR

S onny Longtine, a lifelong resident of Marquette, holds bachelor's and master's degrees from Northern Michigan University and has completed additional graduate work at Eastern Michigan University and Michigan State University. He was in public education for thirty-three years as a political science teacher and a counselor. Sonny has authored *Marquette: Then and Now*; *Michigan's Upper Peninsula: Life, Legends and Landmarks*; and *Courage Burning*.

Visit us at
www.historypress.net
....